DISCOVER INTERNATIONAL LAW

*With Special Attention for The Hague,
City of Peace and Justice*

BY PROFESSOR WILLEM VAN GENUGTEN
DANIELA HEERDT LL.M.
AND PROFESSOR NICO SCHRIJVER

DISCOVER INTERNATIONAL LAW
With Special Attention for The Hague, City of Peace and Justice
BY PROFESSOR WILLEM VAN GENUGTEN, DANIELA HEERDT LL.M., AND PROFESSOR NICO SCHRIJVER

ISBN: 978-94-6240-350-5

More information and documents related to this book can be found at: http://www.discoverinternationallaw.com

Publisher: Willem-Jan van der Wolf

Wolf Legal Publishers (WLP)
P.O. Box 313
5060 AH Oisterwijk
The Netherlands
E-Mail: info@wolfpublishers.nl
www.wolfpublishers.com

All rights reserved. No part of this publication may be reproduced, stored in a retrieval system, or transmitted in any form or by any means, electronic, mechanical, photocopying, recording or otherwise, without prior written permission of the publisher or author. Whilst the authors and publisher have tried to ensure the accuracy of this publication, the publisher and authors cannot accept responsibility for any errors, omissions, misstatements, or mistakes and accept no responsibility for the use of the information presented in this work.

© The authors/WLP 2017

Contents

TABLE OF CONTENTS

LIST OF ABBREVIATIONS

INTRODUCTION — 5

ACKNOWLEDGEMENTS — 13

Chapter 1: International Peace and Security — 17

Chapter 2: International Dispute Settlement — 43

Chapter 3: Private International Law — 65

Chapter 4: International Family Law — 79

Chapter 5: International Economic Law — 97

Chapter 6: International Law and Technology — 117

Chapter 7: International Criminal Law — 135

Chapter 8: International Climate Law — 155

Chapter 9: Human Rights Law — 173

Chapter 10: Law of the Sea — 195

OUTLOOK — 211

ABOUT THE AUTHORS — 215

INDEX — 217

List of Abbreviations

ASEAN	Association of Southeast Asian Nations
AU	African Union
BRICS countries	Brazil, Russia, India, China, and South Africa
CBDR	Common But Differentiated Responsibility
CC	Creative Commons
CDM	Clean Development Mechanism
CER	Certified Emission Reduction Credits
COP	Conference of the Parties
DSB	WTO's Dispute Settlement Body
EC3	European Cybercrime Centre
ECJ	European Court of Justice
ECTC	European Counter Terrorism Center
EEZ	Exclusive Economic Zone
EPO	European Patent Office
EU	European Union
EUROPOL	European Police Office
G7	Group of Seven
GATT	General Agreement on Tariffs and Trade
GCCS	Global Conference on Cyberspace
GHG	Greenhouse gases
HCCH	The Hague Conference on Private International Law
IBRD	International Bank for Reconstruction and Development
ICC	International Criminal Court
ICCPR	International Covenant on Civil and Political Rights
ICESCR	International Covenant on Economic, Social, and Cultural Rights
ICJ	International Court of Justice
ICSID	International Centre for the Settlement of Investment Disputes (World Bank)
ICTR	International Criminal Tribunal for Rwanda

ICTY	International Criminal Tribunal for the former Yugoslavia
IDA	International Development Association
ILO	International Labour Organization
IMF	International Monetary Fund
IOM	International Organization for Migration
IPCC	Intergovernmental Panel on Climate Change
ISFL	International Society of Family Law
ITLOS	International Tribunal for the Law of the Sea
IUU	Illegal, Unreported, and Unregulated (Fishing)
KP	Kyoto Protocol
LRA	Lord's Resistance Army
MFN	Most Favored Nation
MICT	Mechanism for International Criminal Tribunals
NATO	North Atlantic Treaty Organization
NC3A	NATO's consultation, command, and control agency
NCI Agency	NATO Communications and Information Agency
NGO	Non-governmental organization
NIEO	New International Economic Order
NSA	National Security Agency
OAS	Organization of American States
OCTA	European Organized Crime Threat Assessment
OPCW	Organisation for the Prohibition of Chemical Weapons
OSCE	Organisation for Security and Co-operation in Europe
PCA	Permanent Court of Arbitration
PCIJ	Permanent Court of International Justice
PMSC	Private Military and Security Company
R2P	Responsibility to Protect
STL	Special Tribunal for Lebanon
TRIPS	Agreement on Trade-Related Aspects of Intellectual Property Rights
TTIP	Transatlantic Trade and Investment Partnership
UDHR	Universal Declaration of Human Rights
UK	United Kingdom
UN	United Nations
UNCITRAL	United Nations Commission on International Trade Law
UNCLOS	United Nations Convention on the Law of the Sea

UNCRC	United Nations Convention on the Rights of the Child
UNESCO	United Nations Educational, Scientific and Cultural Organization
UNFCCC	United Nations Framework Convention on Climate Change
UNHCR	United Nations High Commissioner for Refugees
UNIDROIT	International Institute for the Unification of Private Law
UNSC	United Nations Security Council
UPR	Universal Periodic Review
USA	United States of America
WHO	World Health Organization
WMD	Weapons of Mass Destruction
WTO	World Trade Organization

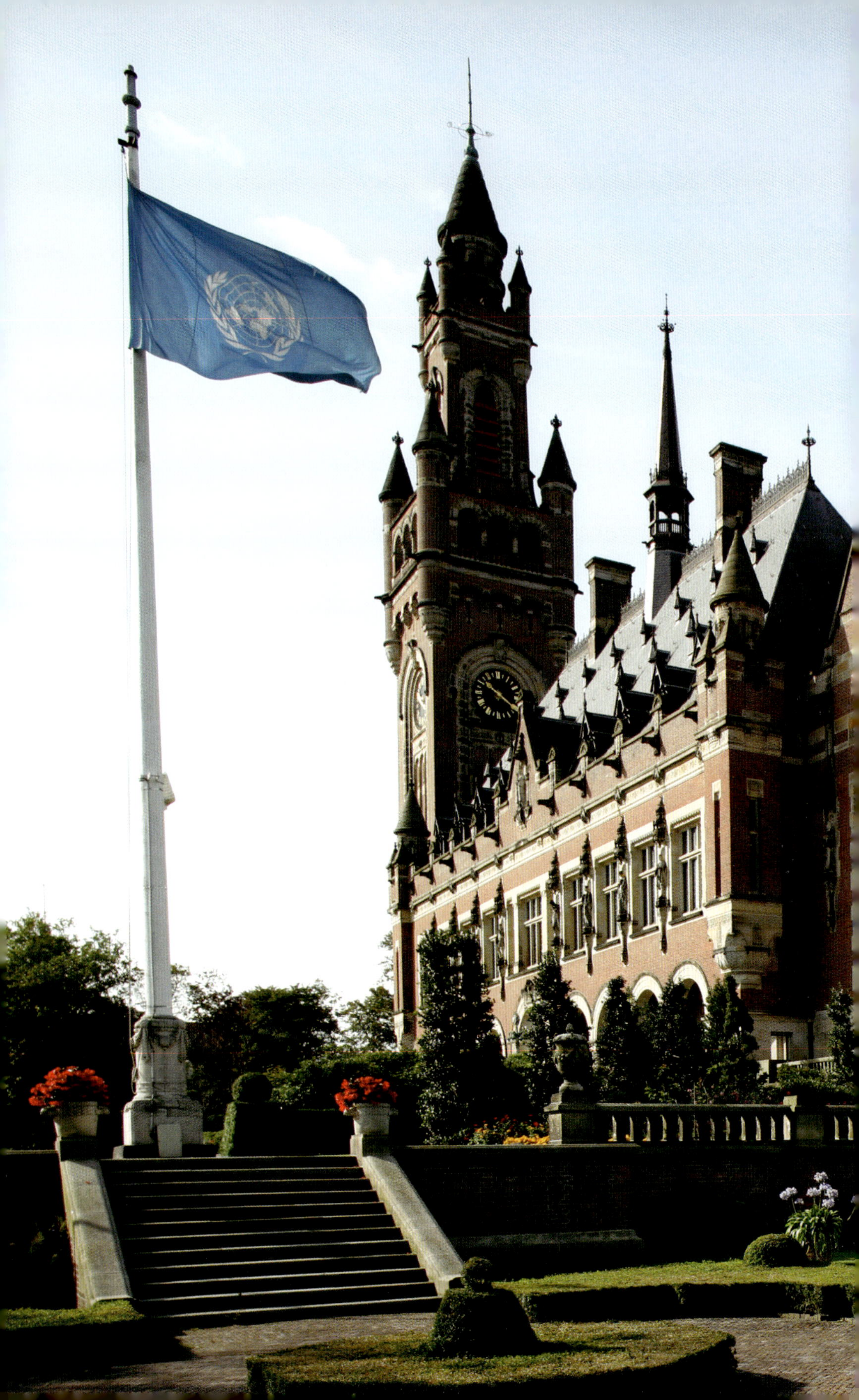

Introduction

Pope Paul VI gives a speech to the U.N. General Assembly, 4 October 19

1. Introduction

International law belongs to everyone and influences the lives of all people worldwide, no matter whether they are aware of that or not. It might relate to armed conflicts, natural disasters caused by climate change, the resulting flows of refugees, the realization of human rights, or to international trade. The list is endless. International law in fact covers almost every aspect of life. It matters for ending wars, for water and food security, and for enjoying freedom of speech. What is more, without international law in the form of agreements between states, we would not even, for example, have a common understanding of how long a second is. We could not enjoy watching foreign TV, nor would people be able to choose from a variety of fruits and vegetables knowing where they come from.

Yet explaining what international law actually is and how it comes about in a simple way is not easy. International law takes many forms and is shaped in various ways. For example, private international law is different from and works differently than public international law, as will be explained in the chapters that follow. Generally speaking, international law is made up of rules that govern the international community to ensure peaceful coexistence of all actors and human dignity for everyone and it does so by addressing current needs and taking away the barriers we come across when we move actively across borders. The United Nations (UN) is the organization working for that cause, and international law is just one channel through which these values and visions can be achieved.

Logo of the United Nations

International law is in many ways different from national law. It's important to understand this. Legal systems within countries are shaped by parliaments or other legislative bodies and based on constitutions, and usually have one central authority that enforces the law. This is not true of international law. No international parliament exists, nor a central executive power and enforcement authority, nor an international constitution, unless you would see the UN Charter that way. However, that "mother document of modern public international law" – as rich and relevant it is – is at best only the beginning of such a global constitution. In fact, states together shape the law they agree to be bound by (the consent to be bound). They do so for the most part voluntarily, as a starting point at least.

That said, two points are important to bear in mind. First is that some parts of international law are binding on states even if they do not consent to be bound. These include the basic rules on genocide, crimes against humanity, war crimes and aggression, and of Chapter VII resolutions on peace and security adopted by the UN Security Council. The latter are also binding for the states that might disagree. Second is that international law is no longer solely the domain of states, even if they are still the first actors to be at the "steering wheel." Making and enforcing international law are increasingly influenced by international and regional organizations, nongovernmental organizations (NGOs), expert bodies, and private parties such as transnational enterprises. These entities also see themselves more and more as co-owners or co-constituents of the international legal order, and as having corresponding rights and obligations. States and the UN cannot do without them. The previous UN Secretary-General Ban Ki-moon recently said in a speech on countering violent terrorism, "governments cannot do it alone. We need to engage all of society – religious leaders, women leaders, leaders in the arts, music and sports." Other actors are needed to fulfil the high ambitions of the UN in domains such as peace and security, social and economic development, the environment, and human rights.

The purpose and goal of this book is to contribute to the understanding of the state of the art of public and private international law, including trends and highlights. It consists of ten chapters on international peace and security, dispute settlement, private international law, family law, international economic law, international law and technology, international criminal law, human rights, climate law and the law of the sea. Some readers will at first sight miss some topics, maybe even their favourites. These might relate to the rights of indigenous peoples, refugee law, international humanitarian law, or the fight against terrorism. Such topics could have been added as separate chapters, but the authors decided instead to integrate them into other chapters.

In each chapter, the book introduces basic concepts of international law, as well as international organizations and historical events that may be relevant for the development of the correspondent field. The book thus provides the reader with a basis for understanding and studying any of the raised issues in more detail. The reader will also develop an understanding of the interconnectedness of the different legal topics and developments. To make reading easier, a glossary explains common terms of international law. The glasses 👓 behind a word indicate that the word can be found in the glossary. With cross references in the margins links between various chapters are indicated 💡. Finally, the most important issues discussed in the texts are being highlighted in color.

A second goal of this book is to present the unique and long-standing relationship between international law and the city of The Hague, "the

U.N. Secretary General Ban Ki-moon at the 100th anniversary of the Peace Palace in The Hague (28 August 2013) calling the city of The Hague: an epicentre of international justice and accountability.

legal capital of the world," as former UN Secretary-General Boutros Boutros-Ghali once called it, to which former UN Secretary-General Ban Ki-moon added in 2013, "an epicentre of international justice and accountability." Since the first and second Hague Peace Conferences in 1899 and 1907, The Hague has developed and become recognized as a forum for knowledge, research, and experience in the field of international law. The city hosts a range of key legal institutions vital to the international legal system. In each chapter, those Hague institutions are presented that have a particular meaning for the development of that particular aspect of international law and that have their official headquarters in the city.

The Hague also maintains, apart from the institutions and organizations formally working in private and public international law, a tradition of staging major international conferences, including the Climate Conference in 2006, the International Conference on Afghanistan in 2009, the Nuclear Security Summit in 2014, and the Cyber Security Conference in 2015. The city's tradition of connecting states and other international actors is more visible than ever today. In 2012, the Supreme Court of the Nobility officially granted the city the right to include the maxim "Peace and Justice" into its coat of arms. To more closely tie the book to the city of The Hague, the authors also decided to interview key players in the field of international law who are active in The Hague.

Participants of the First Hague Peace Conference, May-July 1899, in House of the Woods.

The Kingdom of the Netherlands in general is a vital player in the field of international law. According to Article 90 of the Dutch Constitution, the government of the Netherlands is obliged to "promote the development of the international legal order." The city of The Hague, which is the seat of the Dutch government, has taken this constitutional duty to heart. Within the past decade, the number of international governmental and nongovernmental organizations working jointly for a safer and just world by actively promoting the development of international law and the rule of law has more than doubled.

This book does not claim to be a complete collection of public and private international law issues. It rather reflects on current global challenges and their connection to international law in selected domains. It was finalized in the summer of 2016 and some of the information provided is time sensitive. Nevertheless, this book should provide the reader with a general understanding of what international law is all about, which is timeless knowledge. The online version of this book (www.discoverinternationallaw.com) includes links to up-to-date online information on the issues addressed.

Secretary-Generals of the United Nations 1945-2016.

Gladwyn Jebb 1945 – 1946

Trygve Lie 1946 – 1952

Dag Hammarskjöld 1953 – 19

U Thant 30 1961 – 197

Kurt Waldheim 1972 – 1981

Javier Pérez de Cuéllar 1982 –

Boutros Boutros-Ghali 1992 – 1996

Kofi Annan 1997 – 2006

Ban Ki-moon 2007 – 2016

Acknowledgements

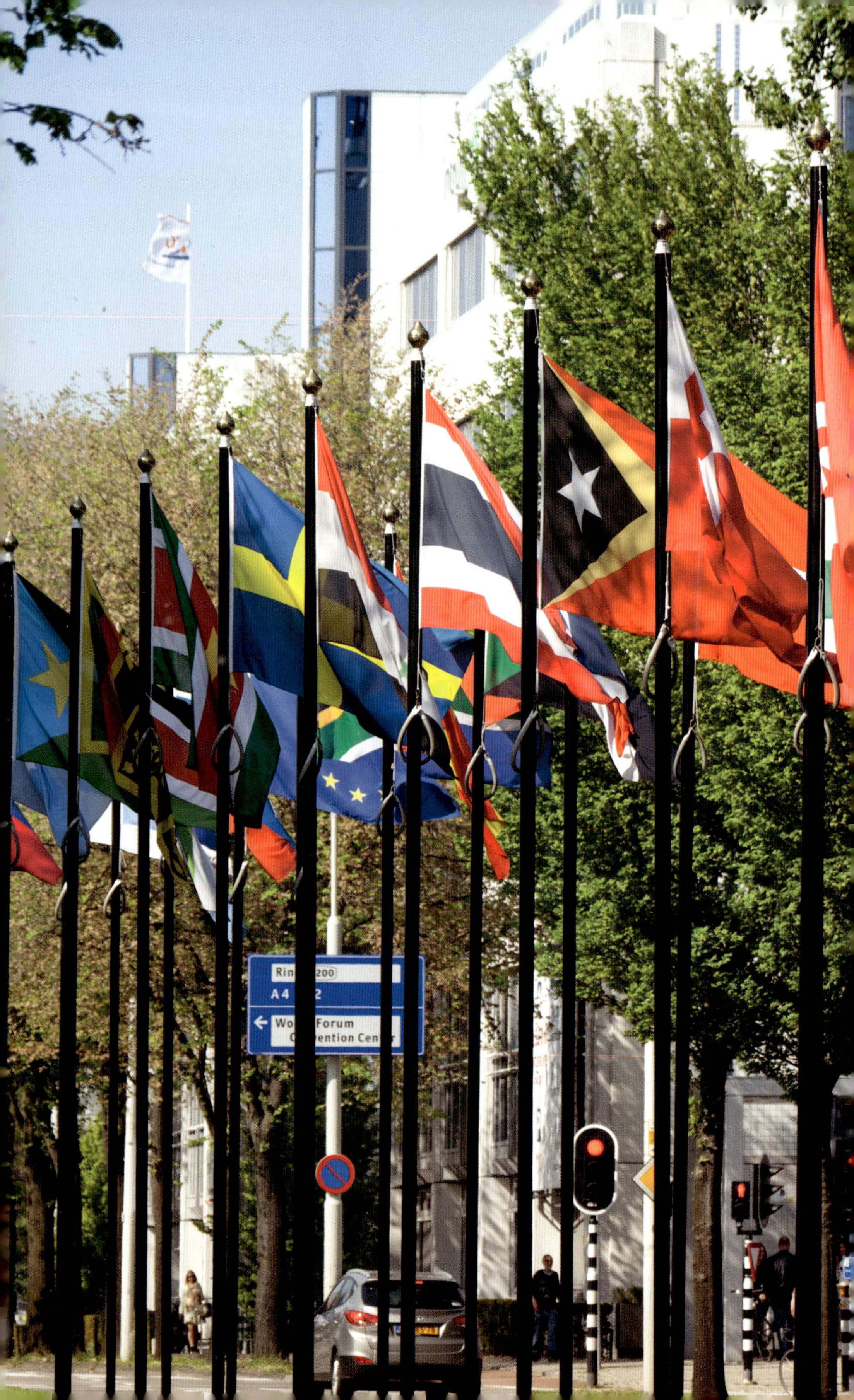

Acknowledgements

Legal debates, those on international law included, are often highly technical, thus running the risk that many people interested in the outcomes are excluded. However, international law should not be a closed shop, with lawyers as its only clients. Against this background, it was decided to write a book accessible to whomever has an interest in international law and who might get lost in a traditional legal handbook. The idea came up in conversations with the municipality of The Hague a few years ago and became concrete in late 2013 at the time of the celebrations of Hundred Years Peace Palace in The Hague. At that moment a plan was presented to the municipality of The Hague and discussed in much detail with Astrid Bronswijk, head of the department of International Affairs of the city, followed by funding by the municipality and next to that by the Royal Netherlands Society of International Law. The funding offered the opportunity to appoint Daniela Heerdt, asking her to draft chapters in each domain to be included in the book.

To gather additional information on recent trends and to pay tribute to the special place that the city of The Hague has gained and continues to gain in some of the fields the book addresses, in 2014 and 2015 interviews were held with then President of the International Court of Justice Peter Tomka, President of the International Criminal Court Sang-Hyun Song, President of the International Criminal Tribunal for the Former Yugoslavia Theodor Meron, Secretary-General of the Permanent Court of Arbitration Hugo Siblesz, and the legal advisor to the Dutch Ministry of Foreign Affairs, Liesbeth Lijnzaad. All of them provided very valuable inputs on a range of issues within their respective fields of work. Sometimes they are quoted and sometimes they are present in an invisible way.

Apart from their input, each chapter has undergone two types of checks. The first relates to the accessibility of the terminology, given that the book is written for a broader lay public. That role has been fulfilled by staff members and interns of the International Affairs Office of the city of The Hague: Nabil Benali, Cunera van den Boorn, Tessa Daling,

13: Man Writing a Letter by Gabriël Metsu.

Heddy Dijk, Aernout Kolijn, Soraya Santhalingam and Stella Visser (names in alphabetical order). We owe them a great deal indeed. The second relates to experts, colleagues in private and public international law, who agreed to look carefully at the chapters while accepting that reaching a lay audience effectively comes with a price. Such roles have been fulfilled, in alphabetical order, by Professors Karin Arts (Institute of Social Studies, The Hague), Niels Blokker (Leiden University), Laura van Bochove (Leiden University), Marcel Brus (Groningen University), Alex Geert Castermans (Leiden University), Hans Franken (em. Leiden University), Larissa van den Herik (Leiden University), Nicola Jägers (Tilburg University), Bert-Jaap Koops (Tilburg University) Vesna Lazic (T.M.C. Asser Institute and Utrecht University), Marta Pertegas (The Hague Conference on Private International Law), Maurice Schellekens (Tilburg University), Jonathan Verschuuren (Tilburg University), Paul Vlaardingerbroek (Tilburg University), Paul Vlas (VU University, Amsterdam), and Harmen van der Wilt (University of Amsterdam). We are extremely grateful that so many colleagues have been willing to help in developing the draft manuscript. The shortcomings, however, including the choices made, remain ours and ours alone.

Willem van Genugten, Daniela Heerdt, and Nico Schrijver,

Tilburg/Leiden, December 2016

International Peace and Security

Soldiers in the Korean War

International Peace and Security

What to expect from this chapter?

One of the major tasks of international law and organizations such as the United Nations (UN) is to prevent conflicts and take measures toward resolution when wars do actually break out. This chapter begins by presenting some of today's threats to international peace and security (part 2), explains the general ban on the use of force under international law and how it came about (part 3), discusses the current security system under the UN framework ⁓ (part 4), and offers possible answers and solutions to current threats (part 5).

1. Introduction

Some people have only heard about armed conflicts in history class or through their grandparents' storytelling. Others live every day in a world of war, either personally or through the media. The ongoing tensions in Syria, Sudan, Nigeria, Afghanistan, Iraq, the Middle East, or the newly formed conflict in Ukraine are but a few recent examples.

2. Threats to International Peace and Security

The number of armed conflicts ⁓ has not in fact decreased since the end of the Cold War. What has changed – and continues to change – is the type of conflict. Most wars today are fought *within* the borders of one state (civil wars). As well as with important issues such as border-crossing terrorism, international law has to deal with a range of threats to international peace and security.

The threat of international terrorism – personified in terrorist or rebel organizations such as al Qaeda, Boko Haram, al Shabaab, or the Islamic State – is one of the most pressing challenges to international law. Although terrorism has been a threat to international peace and security for some time, the number of terrorist groups and attacks worldwide is increasing. One of the challenges for international *law* is that no definition of terrorism has been universally accepted. Some states might identify a certain group as a terrorist organization while other states do not. On the other hand, even if a common definition was reached, legal fights against terrorism would remain problematic because terrorists by definition do not live according to law and neither do the states that support them.

Closely related to international terrorism is organized and cross-border crime ⌇. Open borders and globalization draws the world closer together each day, which makes it easier for criminals or criminal groups to operate across borders. One particularly attractive business is illegal drug trade. Powerful drug cartels often have enormous influence on public life in areas where they are active, leading to corruption and systematic undermining of the power and reliability of governments. Organized crime and terrorism in and of themselves are two major challenges to international peace and security, but they are also symptomatic of other global challenges, such as alarming poverty levels.

Another ongoing risk relates to the existence and use of weapons of mass destruction (WMD) – primarily nuclear, chemical, and biological. The current system of nonproliferation of nuclear weapons (under the Non-Proliferation Treaty) allows the five permanent members of the UN Security Council to have such weapons. Other states are not allowed to have them, as can be seen in the negotiations with Iran, leading to a provisional agreement in early 2015. Concerning the production and use of chemical weapons, a global multilateral ⁓ treaty ⁓ has been in place since 1993, overseen by a supervisory mechanism headquartered in The Hague. As to biological weapons, an international treaty is also in place, since 1972, but it does not include a verification system.

The use of drones as a weapon has expanded in recent years. Drones are unmanned air vehicles used for surveillance or equipped with missiles and bombs and often operated by a person far away from the operational zone. The United States stays ahead of countries that use armed drones in their combat areas. In Europe, several governments are currently planning to buy drones to fight crime. In Eastern Ukraine the Organization for

Security and Co-operation in Europe employs drones to monitor the ceasefire of the Minsk II-peace agreement, of February 2015. Individuals also have easy access to drones and the number of private users grows every day. Some argue that drones revolutionize warfare by offering new possibilities, but use of drones raises not only ethical questions but also numerous concerns on whether it is even legal to use them under international law.

Other threats to international peace and security come in response to social, economic, political, and religious tensions within and between countries. Many conflicts arise from religious intolerance. High levels of poverty and unemployment can lead to both protests against governments and civil wars as well. The revolutions that emerged in the course of the *Arab Spring* since 2010 provide examples for how internal economic or social frustration and political opposition can turn into a revolution that not only disrupts the country but also affects neighboring countries. The 2014 Ukraine crisis is a prime example of how a domestic crisis can turn into a regional and even international conflict that threatens international peace and security. It developed from once peaceful protests for political change at Maidan square to a conflict affecting the entire country, including the loss of territory (the Crimea) and sanctions by the United States and the European Union against the Russian Federation.

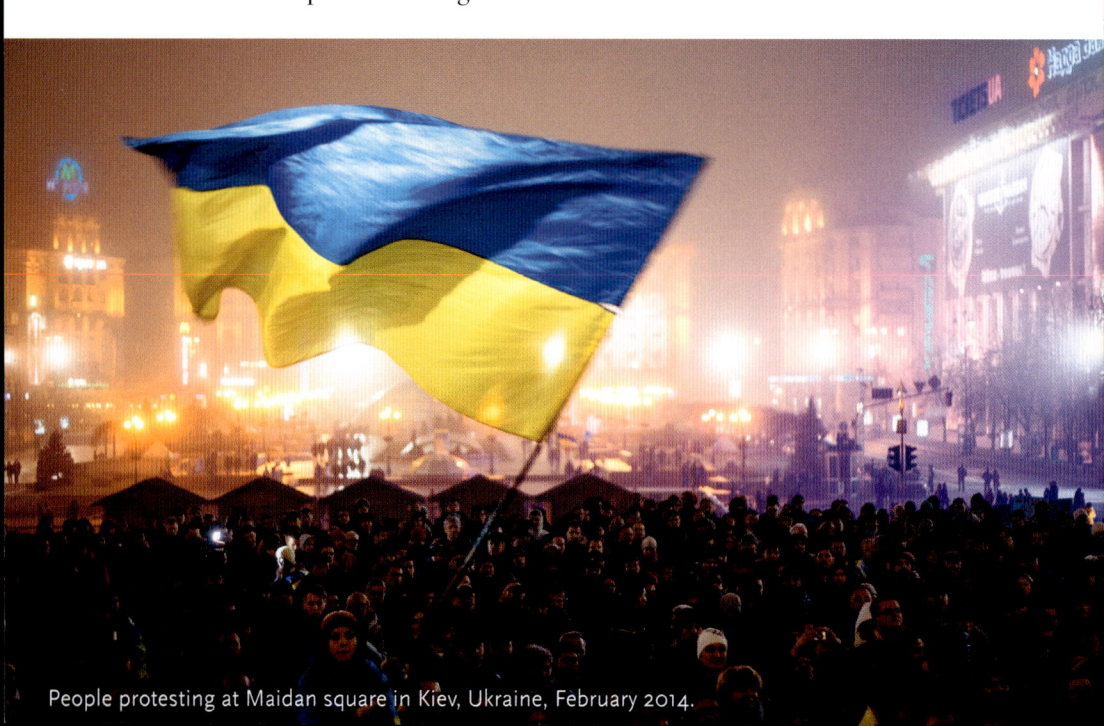

People protesting at Maidan square in Kiev, Ukraine, February 2014.

The Ukraine crisis also shows how important it is to consider the role that media and social media play in today's conflicts. On the one hand, social networks can be helpful in engaging citizens and organizing events. Present-day technologies allow news to travel the world in no time and provide instant information on conflicts. At the same time, they often result in escalating a situation, in particular when media and social networks are used by conflicting parties.

In sum, the world faces threats on many fronts. Even if most of the issues touched on are national threats in first instance, they all still sooner or later can spill over to other countries and become international threats (*spill-over effects*). This is true also of threats posed by climate change or the spread of infectious diseases like Ebola, which can disrupt the stability of entire regions. The resulting flow of refugees is not only a consequence of various threats but also a threat in itself, in that it often leads to further destabilization in the countries to which refugees flee.

The spread of infectious Ebola disease.

Piero Della Francesca, Battle between Heraclius and Chosroes, 1452-66.

3. The Ban on the Use of Force and its Development

International law generally forbids the use of force, even to counter threats such as those defined in this chapter. However, for much of history, states started wars as a political tool. Early attempts to regulate war and the use of force were motivated by religious and moral ideals and resulted in the so-called just war concept. The idea was that war can be justified only if it meets certain criteria, which were determined with respect to the conditions for the right to go to war and for the right behavior in times of war. The *just war* concept has already been used in ancient Rome. Augustine of Hippo, Thomas Aquinas, and Hugo Grotius later refined it. The concept played an essential role throughout history until finally, at the end of the nineteenth century, several states negotiated some restrictions of the use of force at The Hague peace conferences.

p.101

THE MARTENS CLAUSE

A statement by Fyodor Martens (Russian representative at the first and second Hague Peace Conferences) on the status of civilians who take up arms against the occupying forces led to the inclusion of the so-called and nowadays famous "Martens clause" in the preamble of the Hague Convention II. This clause, which states that "populations and belligerents remain under the protection and empire the principles of international law, as they result from the usages established between civilized nations, from the laws of humanity and the requirements of the public conscience", has been restated in the conventions that resulted out of the 1907 peace conference, as well as in the additional protocols to the 1949 Geneva Conventions that deal with international humanitarian law. Although there is no such thing as a generally accepted interpretation of the clause, it is still relevant today. Courts use it as a guideline to understand and interpret existing rules of international humanitarian law.

The First International Peace Conference, May-June 1899.

About The Hague Peace Conferences

... and why some countries did not want to attend

In 1898, Tsar Nicholas II of Russia invited various nations to a conference to discuss disarmament. The invitation was met by great enthusiasm among the members of the so-called peace movement of the time, but opposed by various governments, which did not want to talk about disarmament. But when Fyodor Martens, advisor with the Russian Foreign Ministry and professor of international law, changed the plan for a conference on disarmament into a plan for a conference on peace, the opposition disappeared. The Tsar chose The Hague as a location for the conference because he had family ties with the Dutch royal family and thought that The Hague's central location was convenient for the participants. From May 18 to July 29, 1899, twenty-six countries participated in the First Peace Conference in The Hague, chaired by Tobias Asser and Fyodor Martens. The participating governments adopted a handful of declarations and conventions. One of the real achievements, however, was the foundation of the Permanent Court of Arbitration (PCA).

In 1907, countries were still not willing to talk about disarmament. The Second Hague Peace Conference dealt with the regulation of warfare and resulted in the famous Hague Convention on the Laws of War and War Crimes. The earlier convention was expanded and modified. The conference lasted twice as long as the first and twice as many governments were represented. Despite the failure of a proposal for a court of arbitral justice and international prize court, the second conference again contributed to the development of public international law and the important role played by the city of The Hague.

All good things come in threes and thus a third conference was planned. However, the outbreak of the Great War (now known as World War I) in 1914 interrupted the schedule. Nonetheless, in 1915 an unofficial third peace conference was held in The Hague in 1915. It was quite different from the first two, on the one hand, because it was held under the leadership of the International Women's Movement, on the other because the agenda differed from that of the previous two conferences. Participants drafted a document titled "Principles of a Permanent Peace" that foresaw a number of principles that today are seen as important features of the international law system on peace and security.

British Women's Peace Delegation to the unofficial Third Peace Conference in the Hague, 1915.

The official opening ceremony of the League of Nations, Geneva, 15 November 1920.

After the Hague peace conferences, the next big step in the development of the ban on the use of force was taken in 1918, at the end of World War I. At this point, the use of force as a right of states was somewhat reduced. Still, the founding treaty (also called covenant ⮎) of the League of Nations, the international body created after the end of the war, included no general ban on the use of force. That system is best described as geared toward preventing war, given that declaring war was still lawful for a state after peaceful ways to settle the dispute had been exhausted. The difference was that peace was for the first time seen as a general condition of the international system and war the exception for which justification was needed. Taking this one step further, the famous *Kellogg-Briand-Pact* from 1928 (officially known as the General Treaty for the Renunciation of War) finally banned war altogether as an instrument of national policy. The pact is still valid today, but the ban is limited to war. Other forms of violent action are not included. This situation, however, changed with the founding of the United Nations (UN) at the end of World War II.

Did you know that...

Tobias Asser (born 28 April 1838 in Amsterdam, died 29 July 1913 in The Hague) is the only Dutchman to win a Nobel Peace Prize?

Tobias Asser's family had a long tradition in the field of law. After he had finished his law studies, he became a professor of international and commercial law. He was preoccupied with private international law and managed to convince the Dutch government to host several conferences in that domain. He presided over these conferences in 1893, 1894, 1900, and 1904. Asser was also the Dutch delegate for the two Hague conferences in 1899 and 1907. In addition, Asser had a post as minister until he died in July 1913. In 1911, not long before his death, Asser was granted the Nobel Peace Prize as co-winner for his efforts to establish the Permanent Court of Arbitration and his dedication to solve issues arising from conflicts in the field of private international law.

Why is he important for international law and The Hague?

Tobias Asser is often referred to as the Grotius of his time. His numerous writings and actions helped the city of The Hague become a center for international legal affairs. His interests were broad. He co-initiated The Hague Conference on Private International Law and was a member of the panel that dealt with the first case in front of the PCA. Since 1965, The Hague has hosted the Asser Institute, which is active in both academic research and education in international and European law.

The signing of the Charter of the United Nations and the Statute of the International Court of Justice, San Francisco, 26 June 1945.

4. The United Nations Security System

In October 1945 the Charter of the United Nations entered into force. The content and *principles* expressed in the Charter were inspired on the Four Freedoms developed by U.S. President Franklin Roosevelt in his famous speech from 1941: freedom of expression, freedom of worship, freedom from want, and freedom from fear. The Charter contains various articles on the rights and duties *(obligations)* of UN member states and on the enforcement of international law. Today, 193 countries have accepted the Charter and became members of the UN. The Charter is considered to be one of the main sources of modern international law.

The most important article in the charter with regard to international peace and security is *Article 2*. In paragraph 4 it states,

> *All members shall refrain in their international relations from the threat or use of force against the territorial integrity or political independence of any state, or in any other manner inconsistent with the Purposes of the United Nations.*

This phrasing is a major change from earlier attempts to regulate and ban war. In choosing the word *force* rather than *war*, the drafters of the Charter chose a broader approach that enables the UN to challenge a state's violent action without the action being a war in legal terms. Such a phrase is necessary because nowadays countries no longer formally declare war. In addition, this article in so many words forbids not only the use of force, but also the threat of force. This means that no actual violence needs to occur for a state to breach its obligations under the UN Charter.

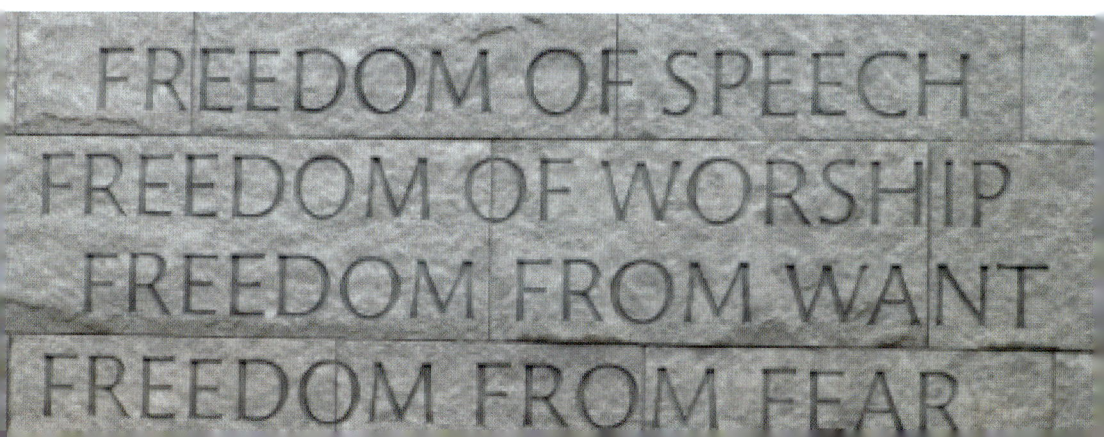

How does the system work?

International law allows *two exceptions* to the general ban on the use of force:

>**One**: An authorization of the use of force by the UN Security Council (UNSC)

The UN organ with the primary responsibility for collective security and hence to maintain international peace and security, the Security Council is made up of five permanent members with veto power: China, France, Russia, the United Kingdom, and the United States. If one of these five objects to (vetoes) a certain proposal, the proposal cannot be adopted. In addition, ten nonpermanent members have a vote but their negative votes cannot prevent a resolution from being adopted. They are elected for a two-year term. More than sixty UN member states have never been a member of the Security Council.

The United Nations Security Council.

An authorization of the use of force is done through adopting a *resolution* for which nine of fifteen votes are necessary, including those of all permanent members. In the meantime, however, if permanent members abstain from voting, a resolution can still be adopted as long as nine of fifteen members vote in favor. Before the Security Council can authorize any measure, it must identify a threat to the peace, breach of the peace, or act of aggression.

After having established that that is the case indeed, the Security Council can take several measures. It can decide on economic or diplomatic sanctions, or it can decide to launch a military intervention. In past years, the Council increasingly used *smart* or *targeted sanctions* rather than *comprehensive sanctions*. Smart or targeted sanctions are in most cases aimed at certain individuals, such as travel bans or freezing of personal assets. Their advantage is that they do not affect the entire population, which has often been the case with comprehensive sanctions, such as against Iraq or the former Yugoslavia. Comprehensive sanctions can be far-reaching economic sanctions, such as the prohibition of all exports or imports.

Smart sanctions have also been under criticism from a human rights perspective, in particular since the Kadi cases before the European Court of Justice (2008, 2010). Kadi, a Saudi-Arabian businessman, was listed as terrorist associate by a UN Security Council resolution and later also by the European Union (EU), whereupon his assets in the United States were frozen. Kadi challenged these acts on the grounds that they violate his rights to property and a fair hearing. He was successful in the EU Court of Justice and his name was removed from that list. Similar cases have been filed by individuals sanctioned in the course of the Russia-Ukraine conflict. Particular outcomes aside, these cases make clear that finding a balance between promoting international peace and security and protecting human rights is critical.

chapter 9

Two: A state's right to self-defense

The UN Charter gives states the right to act in individual or collective self-defense in response to an armed attack. The right is only temporary because states must report their decision to use force to the Security Council and have the right only until the Security Council steps in.

The sinking of the steamboat Caroline, 1837.

In the *Nicaragua* case, from 1986, the International Court of Justice (ICJ) in The Hague ruled that the measures taken in response to an attack must be proportionate, meaning that states may do only enough to defend against the attack, nothing more. In quite a few cases, however, this is difficult to establish, in particular with regard to "new" threats, such as terrorist attacks. Here, the difference between *preventive* and *anticipatory* (or *preemptive self-defense*) is relevant. Whereas 'anticipatory' refers to action in the context of a situation that meets criteria such as "instant and overwhelming threat, and leaving no choice of means and no moment for deliberation" (the so-called '*Caroline doctrine*' from 1837), 'preventive' refers to action taken at the moment the threat is more remote. Whereas anticipatory self-defense is near acceptance by large parts of the international community, preventive self-defense is not, as the ICJ confirmed in the Nicaragua case.

What other systems are there?

Overall the UN system of peace and security can be described as a system of collective security ⌒: the security of one state is the concern of all. The North Atlantic Treaty Organization (NATO), founded in 1949, takes a slightly different approach. NATO is a regional organization whose goal is to safeguard the freedom and security of its twenty-eight members using political and military methods under a system best be described as collective self-defense. To protect the security of its members effectively, NATO constantly updates its defense plans. After the 2014 Ukraine crisis, NATO once again adapted its collective defense measures by preparing additional military responses and testing the readiness of its forces. The UN also regularly engages NATO to assist in handling different crises.

NATO's consultation, command, and control agency (formerly NC3A, now NCI Agency) is located in The Hague. It provides communications and information systems, as well as IT support to NATO headquarters, the NATO command structure, and NATO agencies. This includes developing technology, experimenting, promoting architecture design and engineering, testing, and providing technical support.

NATO at its 50-years celebration Washington Summit, 1999.

In addition, the NATO CIMIC Center of Excellence (CCOE), one out of eighteen centers of excellence established by NATO, is also hosted in The Hague. It is an international military center of expertise, working for the cause of military-civilian cooperation by providing advice and expertise in the development of policies and trainings. Its formation was triggered by the conflicts in the Balkans in the 1990s.

Did you know that ...

NATO Communications and Information Agency (NCI Agency) has more than twenty-five locations spread across Europe, North America, and South-East Asia?

Established:	2012
Main activities:	Strengthens NATO through connecting its forces, delivering secure, coherent, cost-effective and interoperable communications and information systems services in support of consultation, command and control and enabling intelligence, surveillance and reconnaissance capabilities
Website:	http://www.ncia.nato.int

NATO Communications and Information Agency
Agence OTAN d'information et de communication

NCIA is partner of The Hague Security Delta, which is the largest security cluster in Europe.

5. Answers to Current Threats

Over the years, states and both international and regional organizations have developed different strategies and tools to address current threats to worldwide peace and security: some are *reacting* to existing threats; others are more *preventive* in identifying a threat and stopping before a conflict develops. When attempting to prevent a conflict, it is essential to look at the main reasons (*root causes*) of the conflict, which are different for each country and each conflict.

What are the strategies and tools available? A selection:

Diplomacy, the practice of state representatives negotiating on certain issues, is a *conflict prevention* tool in improving communication between countries and delivering updates about latest developments. This supports the identification and evaluation of threats. A number of international and regional organizations developed early-warning mechanisms to help diagnose threats at the earliest possible stage. Preventing new conflicts after a conflict has ended is also important, integral to which is seeing whether states are living up to the agreements reached to end the conflict (*compliance* ⬀). One entity particularly active in conflict prevention is the *Organisation for Security and Co-operation in Europe* (OSCE), which also focuses on a variety of other crisis-related issues. It sent, for example, a special monitoring mission to investigate the outbreak of the 2014 Ukraine crisis and was active in deescalating the *humanitarian crisis* in Syria. The OSCE is based on what are called the Helsinki Principles, which are grouped into three baskets:
- peace and security,
- economic and environmental issues, and
- human rights and democracy.

A special wing of the OSCE is the Office of the High Commissioner on National Minorities, located in The Hague.

p. 189

Europol is another European organization involved in conflict prevention, though it in fact combines preventive and reactive strategies. Established by the Europol Convention of 1998, it was continued – with certain changes – under an EU Council decision in 2010. Since 1999, Europol has been based in The Hague and since 2011 it is active in its new headquarters in fighting drug trafficking, illegal immigration networks, human trafficking, child pornography, financial crime, and cybercrime, among others. Using its advanced European Organized Crime Threat Assessment (OCTA), Europol identifies and evaluates emerging threats. It works closely with law enforcement agencies of the twenty-eight EU member states and maintains close connections with other partners outside the EU.

Did you know that ...

Europol has one of the largest concentrations of analytical capabilities in the EU, carrying out more than eighteen thousand cross-border investigations each year?

> In January 2016, Europol launched the European Counter Terrorism Center (ECTC).

Established: 1999 (fully operational)
Mandate: Supports law enforcement authorities throughout the EU on crime fighting activities in all its mandated areas
Structure: Director (assisted by 3 deputy directors), Operations Department, Governance Department, Capabilities Department
Website: https://www.europol.europa.eu/

INTERNATIONAL PEACE AND SECURITY | 39

Did you know that ...

the Organisation for the Prohibition of Chemical Weapons (OPCW)'s working staff represents seventy nationalities?

Established:	1997
Main activities:	Promotes and verifies the adherence to the Chemical Weapons Convention, which prohibits the use of chemical weapons and requires their destruction
Structure:	Conference of the State Parties, Executive Council, Technical Secretariat, and Subsidiary Bodies
State Parties:	192
Official languages:	English, French, Russian, Chinese, Spanish, Arabic
Website:	https://www.europol.europa.eu/

In contrast to Europol and its broad approach, the Organization for the Prohibition of Chemical Weapons (OPCW) focuses on a particular issue: the threat posed by chemical weapons. In 1993, the Convention on the Prohibition of Development, Production, Stockpiling, and Use of Chemical Weapons and Their Destruction was adopted to end the continuing use of chemical weapons in conflicts. Almost all countries in the world are parties to the convention. The adoption brought about the establishment of the OPCW and its headquarters in The Hague. The primary OPCW aims are monitoring nonproliferation of chemical weapons, collecting evidence of the destruction of existing chemical weapons, giving assistance and protection to all members, and promoting international cooperation in peaceful chemistry. It is a fully independent organization that has almost reached its goal of universal membership. The OPCW has close working relations with the United Nations on the removal of chemical weapons from Syria, among other issues.

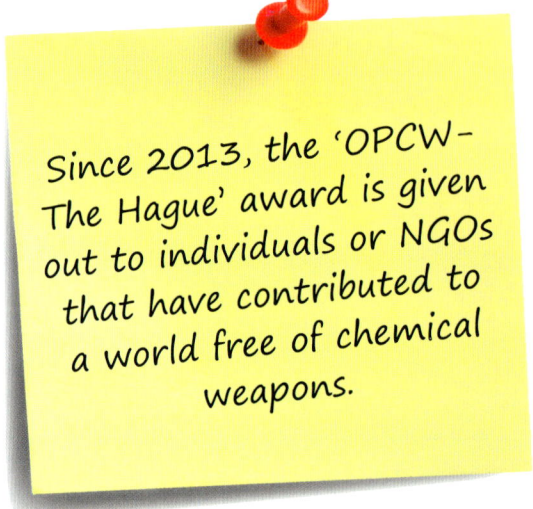

> Since 2013, the 'OPCW-The Hague' award is given out to individuals or NGOs that have contributed to a world free of chemical weapons.

Another response to international peace and security threats is the UN's activity in the field of *peacekeeping*. Peacekeeping means sending armed forces, known as blue helmets, into the territory of a state with the state's approval to monitor peace or act as a buffer between fighting parties. These blue helmets are not allowed to use force except in self-defense, for which they carry light weapons. Since 1948, the UN has initiated sixty-nine operations, sixteen of which are still active in places such as Mali, Afghanistan, and Haiti. Over the decades, the tasks of these operations slightly changed. Current peace operations are often related to governance issues, such as decision-making, participation, transparency, or building stable structures and institutions. These efforts are also known as post conflict peacebuilding. In such situations, it is again important to take the root causes of the conflict into account and to work jointly with local, regional, and national people and organizations to ensure the success of these operations.

In addition to these practical responses, different concepts have developed that focus on how to address today's conflicts. One is humanitarian intervention ⁊, defined as military action taken by a state or a group of states against another state without the authorization of the Security Council to respond, for example, to gross and systematic human rights violations. The concept is highly problematic because it contrasts two international law principles: that of state sovereignty ⁊ and that of protecting innocent civilians under international law. Still, the concept plays a role, which demonstrates a growing awareness that sovereignty is not an absolute right of states and that a balance between sovereignty and the respect for human rights is critical.

Under the concept of Responsibility to Protect (R2P), which the UN developed and its General Assembly adopted in 2005, the international community has the responsibility to protect people if a state itself is not doing so. If the state fails to protect its people, the international community might, as a first step, interfere with advisors. Military intervention is a measure of last resort. The difference to the non-authorized humanitarian interventions is that use of R2P needs Security Council approval. Resolution 1973, adopted in 2011 and authorizing the use of 'all necessary means' to protect civilians and civilian populated areas in Libya, is seen as the first case in which the Council authorized the use of force under R2P.

Finally, and returning to Roosevelt's Four Freedoms, especially the freedom from fear, is the concept of human security. All kinds of threats and challenges can cause fear among people, be it terrorist acts, organized crime, weapons of mass destruction, social or economic crises, political instability, the spread of infectious diseases, environmental catastrophes, or a combination of these. Looking at peace and security through the lens of human security can above all make clear that human beings are and should be at the center of any action in the domain of international peace and security.

International Dispute Settlement

Inside the International Court of Justice.

International Dispute Settlement 2

What to expect from this chapter?

Methods of dispute settlement are the topic of this chapter. Parts 2 and 3 present the various ways to settle legal disputes, discussing arbitration — which, alongside negotiation, is one of the oldest ways to solve disputes — in more detail. Part 4 deals with the International Court of Justice and its development. Part 5 discusses the various challenges that courts of international law are facing today.

1. Introduction

Disputes arise in everyday life, in every society, everywhere on the planet. On an international level, a legal dispute is a disagreement on the interpretation or application of a rule of international law between two or more international actors, which in some instances can turn into a *conflict*, on occasion even an armed conflict. That is why international law has developed, over the last few centuries, different methods to peacefully settle such disputes to avoid outbreak of violent conflict.

2. Peaceful Dispute Settlement

According to Article 2, paragraph 3 of the UN Charter, all members

> shall settle their international disputes by peaceful means in such a manner that international peace and security, and justice, are not endangered.

43: International Court of Justice, chaired by then President Rosalyn Higgins (2006-2009).

Article 2 underscores the connections between peace, security, justice, and dispute settlement. Extending it, Article 33 mentions the methods by which states should settle their disputes:

> *The parties to any dispute, the continuance of which is likely to endanger the maintenance of international peace and security, shall, first of all, seek a solution by negotiation, enquiry, mediation, conciliation, arbitration, judicial settlement, resort to regional agencies or arrangements, or other peaceful means of their own choice.*

The U.N. Charter as signed in 1945.

These methods all differ from one another. The first four – negotiation, enquiry, mediation, conciliation – are *non binding*, that is, the outcome of the dispute settlement is not legally binding on the parties. They are also known as *diplomatic* methods.

How do these methods work?

Negotiation, sometimes also called *diplomatic negotiation*, or *good offices*, refers to discussions that both sides have agreed on without bringing in a third party to assist. Such negotiations are typical in the day-today business of international relations. They can also be used to solve a specific legal dispute between parties and are by far the most common way to solve disputes. Enquiry (inquiry), in contrast to negotiation, does lead to the appointment of an independent third party, which can be an individual or a commission. This third party deals with establishing the facts at the basis of the conflict. Enquiry is a method that the UN Human Rights Council, to take one example, often uses, especially on its fact-finding missions to investigate allegations of human rights violations. Mediation also involves an impartial third party who assists the disputing parties in reaching a settlement, the difference being that a mediator has a more active role. Mediation is often used in resolving international trade disputes. Mediation and enquiry come together in conciliation. This form of dispute settlement is again often used in trade disputes but also in other international commercial disputes. Again, the result is not binding on the parties unless they agree to it at the beginning of the settlement.

UN Human Rights Council meeting in Geneva.

3. International Arbitration

Arbitration is seen as one of the successful forms of dispute settlement. Along with determining their own procedural law ✍, the disputing parties can agree on further conditions before the start of the arbitration process, such as the substantive law ✍ to be applied. This flexibility – as Hugo Siblesz, secretary-general of the Permanent Court of Arbitration (PCA), emphasizes it – is also what makes arbitration so popular. The outcome is not only legally binding but also final.

International commercial arbitration is the most common type and is regularly intended to resolve business disputes between private parties. However many arbitration cases relate to investment claims between states and investor companies. The PCA currently serves as registry for more than fifty *investor-state arbitrations*, one of which is a case between the US-based Windstream Energy LLC and the government of Canada. In 2013, Windstream instituted proceedings against the Canadian government for lost profits. The company claims that the government's action of stopping all offshore projects because of the outcome of an environmental impact assessment has frustrated development of the investment project.

Unlike negotiation, enquiry, mediation, and conciliation, arbitration is legally binding on the parties to a dispute. And while states are well accustomed to resolving disputes by arbitration, in recent decades more and more nonstate actors ✍ (such as multinational enterprises) have come to play a role in international law, leading to an increase of the number of legal disputes between states and nonstate actors. Arbitration is not only one of the most commonly used forms of dispute settlement; it is also one of the oldest. Given its long tradition, it is a universally recognized practice. The first permanent international dispute settlement mechanism, established in 1899 at the first Hague Peace Conference, was the Permanent Court of Arbitration.

Despite its name, the PCA is not a court but rather an international organization ✍ that provides arbitrators ✍ and services for settling disputes and a registry that can serve as the secretariat of arbitral tribunals.

Did you know that ...

The Permanent Court of Arbitration offers four of the dispute settlement methods recommended in the UN Charter (arbitration, mediation, enquiry, and conciliation?

Established:	1899
Mandate:	Provides services for the peaceful resolution of disputes between states, state entities, intergovernmental organizations, and private parties
First Case:	May 1902, Pious Fund of the Californias (US v Mexico)
Number of cases dealt with:	More than 250
State Parties:	117
Official languages:	English and French
Website:	http://www.pca-cpa.org/

It was established by the 1899 Convention for the Pacific Settlement of International Disputes and was a major step in the development of the "peace through law" movement. It also marked the starting point for The Hague's reputation as an international center for peace and justice. Moreover, it was agreed during the negotiations on the convention that the PCA deserved a suitable building in which it could host future peace conferences, which led to the construction of the Peace Palace.

In its early years, the PCA resolved a range of international disputes. With the arrival of the *Permanent Court of International Justice (PCIJ)* after the end of World War I, however, the activity of the PCA gradually declined. Over recent decades, this trend has reversed, in part because of changes in the types of cases brought. Today, cases involve a mix of states, private parties, and intergovernmental organizations.

The original design of the Peace Palace by Cordonnier.

Construction of the Peace Palace, 1907-1913.

About the Peace Palace
and why there would be no Peace Palace without a library

In 1907, at the second Hague peace conference, the first stone was laid for the new home of the PCA: the Peace Palace. The French architect Louis Cordonnier (1854–1938) won the international competition for its design, which had been suggested by the Scottish-American industrialist and philanthropist Andrew Carnegie (1835–1919). Carnegie, after some persuasion, donated $1.5 million for the construction of the palace, with one condition: a library would be integrated in the project to provide the PCA with standard literature on international law.

The construction phase of the palace took six years. Along the way, countries from around the world contributed by donating building materials or decorations, such as windows, the steel gate, and the clockwork mechanism. The Peace Palace finally opened its doors in 1913. The opening ceremony was attended by Queen Wilhelmina and honored Andrew Carnegie for his outstanding support. The same day, the library also opened its doors. Today, the library is one of the oldest and most prestigious libraries in international law. Anyone with an interest in international law is invited to use it.

Although the Palace was criticized at its opening for being too large, within a decade it proved to be too small. In 1922, a new tenant arrived: the Permanent Court of International Justice, predecessor of the International Court of Justice. A year later, The Hague Academy of International Law, a center for research and teaching public and private international law also moved in. In 2007, a new conference center with state-of-the-art technology was added. The Carnegie Foundation continues to be responsible for managing the premises and the building. Since construction began, the Peace Palace has been an icon for The Hague as an international center for peace and justice.

Andrew Carnegie

Other international tribunals also deal with arbitration cases. One specifically designed to address claims between state parties and nationals of the states is the Iran-US Claims Tribunal, established in 1981 in response to the Iranian revolution and US hostage crisis of 1979. That year, when fifty-two Americans were taken hostage in the US embassy in Tehran (a crisis featuring in Ben Affleck's 2012 film *Argo*), the government in Washington reacted by freezing Iranian assets and imposing economic sanctions. Iran in turn reacted by seizing American property rights in Iran. In 1980, the US military landed in Iranian territory in an attempt to rescue the hostages, but failed to do so. The Algerian government stepped in as mediator, which led to the founding of the Iran–US Claims Tribunal.

Visual of the film Argo on the US-Iran crisis

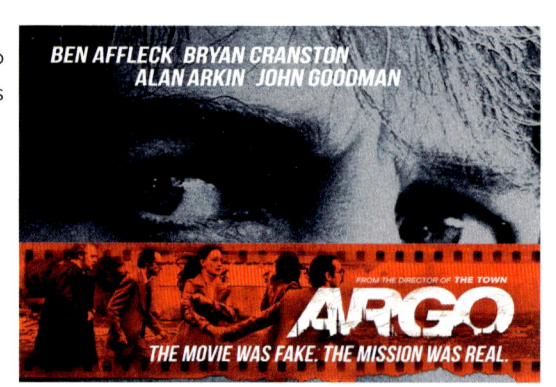

US hostages in Tehran, 1979

Did you know that ...

The Iran-US Claim Tribunal so far dealt with almost four thousand cases?

Established:	1981, by Iran and the United States
Main activity:	Resolve outstanding claims by nationals of one state party against the other – and certain claims between the two states – in relation to the 1979–1981 Iran-U.S. conflict
Jurisdiction:	On claims by nationals of one state against the other state and certain claims between the two states
Members:	9 members, 3 members appointed by each Government and 3 (third-country) members selected by the 6 government-appointed members
Official language:	English and Farsi
Website:	http://www.iusct.net/

Both governments agreed to set up an arbitral body in The Hague with the power to hear and decide on all claims by US and Iranian citizens against the other state. These might arise from debts, contracts, or any other situations affecting property rights, and included official claims between the two governments. The first meeting took place in the Peace Palace in July 1981. Since 1982, the tribunal has operated from its own premises. After about thirty-five years, the successful conclusion of the tribunal is now foreseeable.

What is the critique on arbitration?

Arbitration is often said to lack transparency because the involved parties can decide to keep their proceedings private. This criticism is especially relevant when the public interest is at stake. With regard to trade disputes and arbitration, the UN Commission on International Trade Law (UNCITRAL) attempted to address this lack of transparency, adopting new rules in 2014 to make trade arbitration more public and accessible.

Arbitration is often quite costly. High costs, in fact, make arbitration an attractive business. Real arbitration hubs are popping up worldwide. The PCA has reacted to these developments by offering its services outside as well as inside the Netherlands. That more and more cases from different legal fields are being brought to the PCA, such as territorial disputes and environmental law cases, shows its continuing relevance and success.

The ICJ buildings and visitor centre

4. The International Court of Justice

The UN Charter also mentions judicial settlement as dispute settlement mechanism which is where the International Court of Justice comes in. The Paris Peace Conference in 1919 officially ended World War I and led to the establishment of the League of Nations, the first international organization specifically designed with the goal of maintaining world peace. One year later, the League established the Permanent Court of International Justice and decided to locate it in The Hague with the PCA in the Peace Palace where it actually started in 1922. The Court took several years to develop, however, and even before it was fully operational, it was already in decline. One reason was that the two major powers at the time, the United States and the Soviet Union, did not participate in either the League of Nations or the Court. The PCIJ had its last public sitting in 1939.

On 24 October 1945, the United Nations (UN) was officially formed, after the coming into force of the UN Charter. Overall, the organization inherited a number of organs and agencies from the League of Nations period and the PCIJ was replaced by the International Court of Justice (ICJ), to become the principal judicial organ of the UN. On the basis of the PCIJ's location in the Peace Palace, the UN decided to house the ICJ there as well. This choice underscored the reputation The Hague had developed, in particular in conflict resolution. The ICJ is one of the main organs of the UN. Its Statute is an integral part of the UN Charter.

How does the Court work?

The ICJ can hear only cases between states. For that, it has general jurisdiction, meaning that it can hear and rule on any legal issue states bring to it. NGOs for instance can pressure their governments to take certain cases to the ICJ. The Court deals, for example, with legal disputes in the domain of land borders, maritime boundaries, territorial sovereignty, use of force, international humanitarian law, and consular or diplomatic relations. Before the Court can hear and rule on a matter,

Did you know that ...

The International Court of Justice is the only main UN organ not headquartered in New York but in The Hague?

Established:	1945, by the UN
Mandate:	Principal judicial organ of the UN; settles, in accordance with international law, legal disputes submitted by states; may give advisory opinions on legal questions referred to it by authorized UN organs and specialized agencies
Jurisdiction:	General and worldwide
First case:	Corfu Channel Case (United Kingdom v. Albania, 1947)
Number of cases dealt with:	161
Number of advisory opinions:	30
Composition:	15 judges elected for 9-year term of office. The Court sits in full composition. Chambers are possible, but not often used.
State Parties:	193
Official languages:	English and French
Website:	http://www.icj-cij.org/homepage/

however, it must first formally establish whether it has the right to do so (*jurisdiction*). This right is granted only if both parties to the dispute have accepted it. The ICJ is an official UN organ, but UN membership does not mean that all member states accept the Court's jurisdiction. Acceptance is separate and can be handled in various ways.

One option is for states to officially say – by unilateral declaration – that they accept the jurisdiction of the Court for any legal dispute with another state if that other state also accepted the Court's declaration. The state can do so by submitting a document, known as a declaration, to the Court. At present, only seventy-two of the 193 UN member states have unilaterally accepted the jurisdiction of the Court as binding *(compulsory jurisdiction)*. Reasons for not accepting to binding jurisdiction are numerous, but usually relate to a governments' wish to decide on a case-by-case basis and not to be bound automatically by a judicial review.

Another possibility is that states that have not submitted a unilateral declaration but still would like the ICJ to hear and rule on their dispute can both agree to refer their case to it. This is also called ad hoc consent or compromis. A state can also accept the jurisdiction of the ICJ by simply showing up when another State has filed a case and the proceedings start *(forum prorogatum)*.

The ICJ has become an active user of social media. It recently created a Twitter account and posts updates for their followers on a regular basis. Their Twitter username is @cij_icj.

Last, quite some treaties include an article explicitly stating that in case of a dispute between parties to the treaty, the matter must be referred to the ICJ. This is the case with the International Convention on the Elimination of All Forms of Racial Discrimination, which Georgia used after the conflict with Russia in 2008. Initially, the Court ordered the parties to not escalate the conflict. Ultimately, though, in 2011 it determined that it did not have jurisdiction and it ruled that the disputing parties must engage in discussions to resolve the dispute before they take it to the ICJ. According to the Court, Georgia had failed to do so.

Once jurisdiction has been established, the proceedings on the merits can begin. The usual procedure can be interrupted if one party raises an *objection*, or if the Court is asked to order protective measures because the rights of one party are still being violated *(interim or provisional measures)*. In some cases, the Court needs to decide on the admissibility of the case, meaning that it looks at whether the case fulfils all the conditions necessary for the Court to rule on it. The proceedings are split into a written phase, in which the disputing states exchange pleadings, and an oral phase, which includes public hearings. The length of the proceedings always depends on the complexity of the case and the cooperation of the parties. Some cases last two to three years, others more than ten. After the hearings, the judges consult with one another and decide by majority. The decision then is presented at a public sitting and is binding on the parties concerned. No appeal is permitted.

Seal of the International Court of Justice.

Judges who do not agree with the majority and the judgment can publish their opinion in a separate document, called a *separate* or *dissenting* opinion. If a judge writes a dissenting opinion, then he or she does neither agree with the majority's decision, nor with the majority's reasoning. If a judge writes a separate opinion, he or she disagrees with the reasoning of the majority but not with the final judgment. Indeed, judges frequently publish such opinions in great detail and at great length. Although some critics argue that dissents can undermine the authority of the Court, dissenting opinions also provide valuable insights into the deliberations.

How is the Court organized?

Normally the Court sits in full session with fifteen judges. The sole nationality requirement is that no two judges can be of the same nationality. Practice has given rise to the habit of filling five of the seats with judges from the permanent member states of the UN Security Council. In general, though, the goal of the Court is to be composed of judges from all continents. If cases arise in which none of the ICJ judges is of the same nationality as the disputing parties, the state or states concerned may appoint someone of their choice as an ad hoc judge. This strategy promotes the political acceptance of the Court and lowers the barriers to submitting cases to it. The impartiality and transparency of the Court are further strengthened by the fact that judgments are always published.

What other functions does the Court have?

In addition to settling legal disputes, the ICJ may also be asked to give its opinion or advice on a particular legal issue, officially called advisory opinion. Such opinions are not legally binding and parties to a dispute are not required to follow the advice, but the opinions can still and often do play an important role in the development of a dispute. This function was first initiated by the PCIJ. The discretion to ask for such an advisory opinion from the Court does not lie with disputing parties, but instead with either the UN Security Council or General Assembly. Specialized

UN agencies, such as UNESCO or the World Health Organization, are also entitled to ask advisory opinions but only with the authorization of the General Assembly and within their fields of competence. Since its inception, the ICJ has delivered some thirty advisory opinions on various aspects of international law, such as the right to self-determination, the legal status of the United Nations as an international organization, and peacekeeping operations.

> **About the ICJ Advisory Opinion "Legal Consequences of the Construction of a Wall in the Occupied Palestinian Territory." and why it did (not) matter:**
>
> *In 2002, Israel began building a wall along its borders with the West Bank, justifying the construction by saying that it was to protect Israeli citizens from outside attacks. The wall, however, had negative impacts on Palestinians: isolating them and limiting their access to fresh water and food. As a result, a debate about the legality of the wall led the UN General Assembly to ask the ICJ for an advisory opinion on the issue. It held that the wall was indeed illegal under several aspects of international law – among them, international humanitarian law, human rights law, and self-defense. In its advisory opinion, the Court invited the UN Security Council and the General Assembly to take further steps to resolve the conflict. Political sensitivities, however, prevented any further action.*

This example aside, the Court's rulings and its advisory opinions can and do indeed strongly influence the development of international law. One question is the extent to which the Court actually creates new law. Officially, the ICJ does not have a law-making role. As Peter Tomka, then President of the ICJ explained in 2014 to the authors of the present book:

"We do not claim to be a law maker; such a role was not assigned to the Court by the UN Charter of which the ICJ Statute is an integral part. We have to be very careful to make rather modest and not bold steps in developing international law because our standing depends on the confidence of states".

Still, numerous ICJ judgments include detailed interpretations and clarifications of certain rules or treaty clauses, creating additional standards or tests to be applied. In addition, in numerous rulings the ICJ finds a particular principle or rule in a treaty to have the status of customary international law, meaning that it is now a rule because states accept it as a rule (*opinio juris*) and behave accordingly (*state*

Wall in the Occupied Palestinian Territory.

practice), even if it is not written law. In a 2010 case between Argentina and Uruguay, for example, the ICJ had to look at a pulp mill constructed by Uruguay on the Uruguay River, which Argentina, backed by public protests and NGOs, then challenged for alleged pollution of the river. The Court ruled that for any major industrial or infrastructural undertaking, an environmental impact assessment and publication of its results are now a requirement under customary international law.

5. New Cases and New Challenges

The Uruguay Argentina case is not the only case related to international environmental law that the ICJ recently dealt with. In March 2014, the ICJ gave its judgment on the Whaling case (*Australia v. Japan: New Zealand intervening*), in which it had to consider considerable scientific data and evidence as well as the ban on whaling. Most cases still concern traditional issues such as maritime zones and treaty interpretation, but the legal issues and types of cases before the ICJ have broadened in recent years.

Ban on Whaling.

The number of international institutions for dispute settlement has risen and existing institutions had to adapt to new developments. The reason is straightforward: new actors and subjects of international law other than national governments need access to international dispute settlement mechanisms. For example, the dispute resolution mechanism developed by the World Trade Organization presents a new way of how international organizations engage in international dispute settlement. Separately, with the establishment of the International Criminal Court, individuals can now be held responsible for their wrongful acts under international criminal law. Relatedly, at the *European Court of Human Rights* in Strasbourg, individuals can also try states for violation of their rights.

p. 104

p. 147

From the establishment of the first judicial settlement bodies to today, much has changed in the way international courts and tribunals are designed and how they function. One thing is clear, however: their existence represents the reliability of international dispute resolution. As Judge Peter Tomka in his time as President of the ICJ said,

> *"Certainly judicial settlement should not be the first option in settling disputes. The majority of disputes could be settled through negotiation or mediation, but judicial settlement should be available as an option because the fact that a dispute might be brought before the Court can have a positive impact on negotiations".*

In interpreting international rules and norms and issuing judgments on violations, international courts bring change to the international as well as the domestic level. Together with their members, they strengthen compliance with their decisions and ultimately strengthen respect for international law generally.

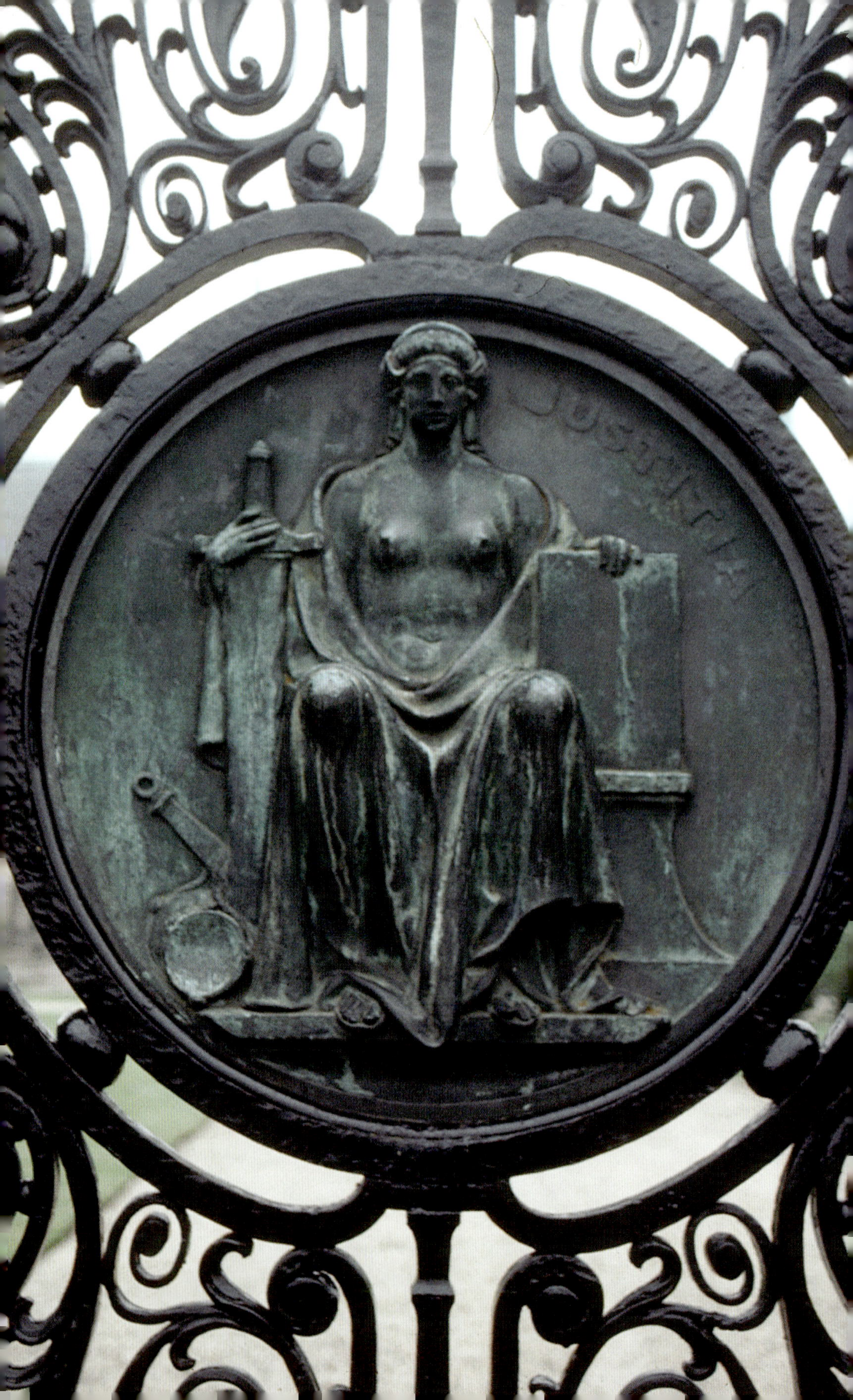

Private International Law

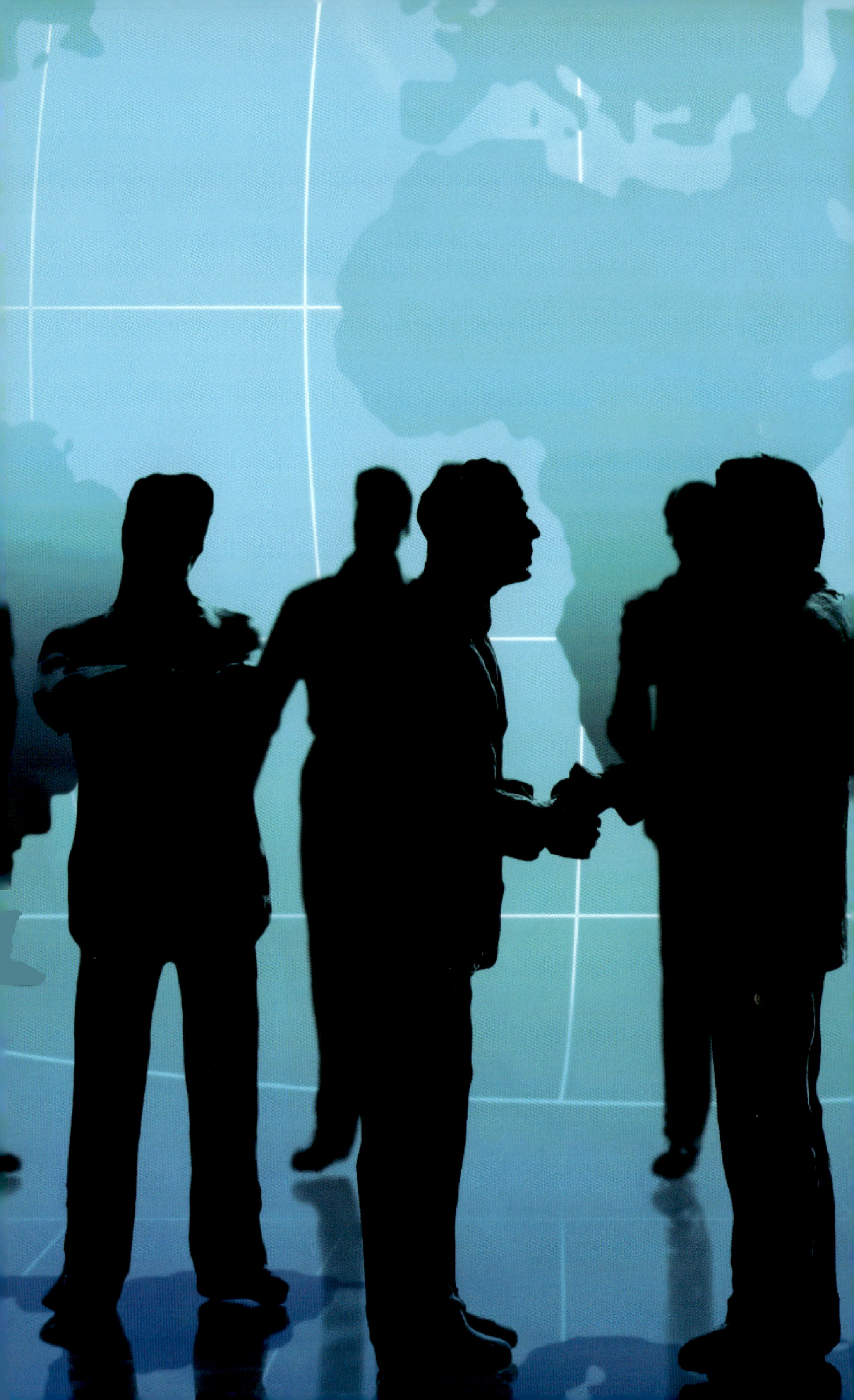

Private International Law 3

What to expect from this chapter?

This chapter illustrates the efforts of states and other entities that have been working together to regulate private international law. In part 2, it deals in more detail with what private international law is all about. Part 3 presents a short historical note on the development of international cooperation in private international law matters. The final parts deal with each of the three main issues of private international law: jurisdiction (part 4), applicable law (part 5) and recognition and enforcement (part 6).

1. Introduction

Private international law is about cases related to more than one legal system, for instance, when the disputing parties do not live in the same country or the dispute concerns property in another country. Rules of private international law deal with **civil** and commercial matters and not with criminal or administrative issues, and are concerned with three main questions. The first is the question of **jurisdiction**, asking which state's court has the legal power to decide on the dispute. The second relates to the law that should be applied. The third is how to recognize and enforce the judicial decision abroad. The word *international* refers to the reach of the dispute that has an international element, even though the dispute itself is a matter of private law.

2. About the Purpose and Function of Private International Law

In the course of globalization of all kinds of activities, more and more relations between private parties also cross national borders. The aim of private international law is to help regulate the legal disputes that arise from **cross-border relations**. Private international law rules are especially needed because different countries have different laws and different legal systems, and different interpretations of both. In a broad sense, it is fair to say that private international law consists of rules that regulate all private cross-border relationships. That the nature of legal relationships under private international law is private does not mean that states are not affected by it, however. In some instances, states can act as a private person (*acta jure gestionis*), such as by handling commercial or investment transactions.

On the flip side, the goal of private international law is not to establish any uniform national law for all countries. Instead, private international law is designed to overcome these differences and to prevent situations in which two courts in two different countries might come up with different decisions on the same case. Private international law rules can or should be thought of as determining which contract law applies to an international contract, testaments, or for instance adoption of children.

What are private international law rules all about?

Private international law can deal with a wide variety of fields as long as a private law question is at the heart of the transaction or relation. These issues can range from family and property law to commercial and finance law and include, for instance, consumer protection or trade-related issues. Private international law operates on the basis of *connecting factors*, which identify which court has jurisdiction over a case and which law should apply to the given circumstances. One such factor is habitual residence, referring to the place where a person lives and regularly returns to or would call home. Other connecting factors also play a role in determining jurisdiction and applicable law, such as where a harmful event occurred.

3. History of Private International Law

Already more than a century ago, the international community started to cooperate in private international law matters. It began at *The Hague Conference on Private International Law* (HCCH, or the Conference), which met for the first time in 1893.

The outcome of the 1893 conference, the first *Hague Convention on Civil Procedure*, was adopted in 1894 and entered into force in 1899, the same year that the first Hague Peace Conference took place. As of 2016,

> The Hague Conference on Private International Law had its sole office in The Hague for 119 years. Since 2012, it has opened regional offices worldwide, beginning with one in Hong Kong and one in Buenos Aires.

Permanent Bureau of the Hague Conference on Private International Law

forty-nine states are contracted to the convention. According to Tobias Asser, who played a leading role in establishing the conference, the aim of those early conferences was to build bridges between the different private law systems.

Apart from the developments in the Hague Conference, another important event in the history of private international law took place in The Hague in 1930: the *Codification Conference*. The event was organized under the patronage of the League of Nations (the predecessor of the United Nations).

About the League of Nations Codification Conference
and why it is relevant for private international law:

From March 13 to April 12, 1930, a number of delegates from different nations came together in the Peace Palace in The Hague to discuss three issues in particular: nationality, territorial borders, and the responsibility of states for damages caused in their territory to a foreign person or property. The objective of the conference was to overcome conflicts in national laws related to these three issues. However, it was clear that this conference alone could not overcome all differences of national laws in the respective areas. Nevertheless, within a month the conference managed to adopt four conventional acts. One was the first international convention ever to be drafted on nationality laws.

In 1955, the Hague Conference became a permanent **intergovernmental organization** ⟡ striving to unify states' private international law rules and general cross-border cooperation in civil and commercial matters. The organization has worked steadily since then to achieve that goal by developing international consensus on approaches to these challenges, such as on the jurisdiction of courts, the applicable law, and the recognition and enforcement of judgments. Through these efforts, the organization responds to current global needs in all private law areas.

Between 1951 and 2008, the Hague Conference adopted thirty-eight conventions. The most ratified are those on **apostille** ⟡ (108 contracting states), child abduction (93 states), intercountry adoption (93 states), conflicts of laws relating to the form of testamentary dispositions (42 states), and child protection (41 states). All of them create rules of private international law that apply to citizens of member and contracting states.

Compared with other international organizations ↝, the Hague Conference has some special characteristics. For one, it creates law. Of all intergovernmental organizations with a legislative function (and these are few), it has the widest reach. It is also active in broadening the network of states bound by one or more of its conventions, creating networks between courts and other authorities across borders. In that regard, the organization works not only with its member states, but also with nonmembers. Importantly, the conventions concluded by the Hague Conference can also be signed and ratified by nonmembers.

Which other actors deal with private international law?

On a regional level, the *European Union* (EU) is one actor especially active in unifying private international law rules for its member states, primarily in form of regulations ↝. Several of these regulations also make reference to HCCH conventions. The most relevant are Brussels I and its recast Brussels I-bis, as well as Brussels II-bis. They again concern the questions of jurisdiction, recognition, and enforcement at the European level, and include divorce and parental responsibility. In addition, the Rome Regulations play an important role in private international law issues within and between EU member states in addressing the question of the applicable law. More on that in part 5 of this chapter.

Similar developments have unfolded in the Americas. The *Organization of American States*, for example, holds specialized conferences on private international law every four to six years. Since the first conference in 1975, it has **adopted** a number of international legal instruments, such as conventions, protocols, or models laws, in the fields of commercial law and family law, among other topics. In Africa, by contrast, the development of private international law is more fragmented. More bilateral treaties than **multilateral** conventions are in place, and most of them deal with recognition and **enforcement** of judgments abroad. In addition, the '*Organisation pour l'Harmonisation en Afrique du Droit des Affaires*' (Organisation for the Harmonization of Business Law in Africa) has since 1993 dealt with private international law issues, particularly in business law.

4. Jurisdiction

When a legal dispute has an international element, it has connections to more than one state and hence also to more than one national **legal system**. This means that more than one state will have the legal power to solve the dispute (jurisdiction). For example, a resident from country A is injured by defective hotel equipment while on vacation in country B. The individual wants to claim damages for pain and suffering. The question is which court to turn to: one in his country of residence, or one in country B? Several factors play into this decision. The **claimant** in this case, for example, should be aware that some countries do not recognize damage claims for pain and suffering.

In the 1990s, the Hague Conference started negotiations on a convention on jurisdiction and recognition and enforcement of judgments. First, the plan was to adopt a broad agreement to deal with all aspects of jurisdiction, as well as all aspects related to enforcing judgments abroad. But in the end, these ambitions were scaled back for lack of consent. The result was the adoption of the *Choice of Court Convention* in 2005, formally the Convention on Choice of Court Agreements. The states parties to the convention must recognize an agreement between disputing parties that expresses their choices of court to hear their case. This agreement can take the form of a contract. The system thus bases jurisdiction on the consent of the parties involved. The chosen court must hear the case and other courts are not allowed to do so. The convention applies to most civil and commercial matters, but expressly excludes consumer and employment contracts. Entered into force in October 2015 for twenty-eight states (Mexico and all EU member states except Denmark), it has been signed by Singapore and the United States as well.

Generally speaking, rules on jurisdiction exist to prevent the disputing parties from *forum shopping*, meaning to choose the court (forum) most likely to decide in the claimant's favor. On the other hand, the purpose is to prevent **parallel litigation** ⚖, that is, the same case being heard by more than one court in more than one legal system. Nevertheless, having parties choose the court to hear their case might not always be the most advisable way forward. Some cases, such as **torts** ⚖, may require special rules. If the parties choose the court, the problem is that only that court may deal with the case, and other courts that might be more suited are not allowed to hear it. Another possibility is for courts to dismiss a case under the *forum non conveniens* doctrine, if the court deems that another court is better suited to hear it. The defendant can also invoke the doctrine.

The decision on which court deals with a certain case is not purely **procedural** ⚖, it is also influenced by the substance of a certain dispute. In general, commercial law issues might require other procedures than family disputes. Also for that reason, it is important for the international community to find common bases of jurisdiction in the different national jurisdiction systems. On the regional level, this was achieved by Brussels I-bis, which applies to questions of jurisdiction in civil and commercial matters in the courts of the EU member states, and Brussels II-bis, which deals with family law matters, such as custody, abduction, or divorce cases.

5. Applicable Law

The next step is to identify which law applies to the dispute, which is also referred to as *choice of law* and can be thought of as a process in which the different laws in question are considered and a decision is taken on which of them applies in the end. For example, imagine a situation in which an employee living in country A suffers an injury while working for a company in country B and now wants to bring claims before a court in country B. The first question is whether this is possible, that is, whether the court has jurisdiction. Next is which law will apply to the dispute. In fact, in cross-border cases on private international law matters, courts often find themselves applying the law of another jurisdiction, at least when the decision is left to the court. This determination can be on grounds of nationality, or on relevance to the dispute. Furthermore, depending on how a certain claim is being characterized, the applicable law can change. This means that if a certain dispute is categorized as a breach of contract, a different law will apply than if it is categorized as tort.

In some cases, the disputing parties have already agreed in a contract which law should apply. This is the case in commercial contracts, where the **principle** ⚭ of *party autonomy* is invoked, meaning that the parties to the dispute decide on the law to be applied. The benefits are that **legal certainty** ⚭ and predictability for the parties are enhanced. This has also been acknowledged by the *Hague Principles on Choice of Law in International Commercial Contracts*, adopted in March 2015. Preparatory work began in 2006; a working group prepared the draft instrument between 2010 and 2014. One of the central aims of the Hague Principles is to promote acceptance of party autonomy for choice of law matters. Interestingly, unlike a convention, the Principles are a **soft law** ⚭ instrument and therefore strictly speaking not legally binding.

The problem with the Principles is that they cover only a part of the general choice of law issue, namely, choice of law for commercial contracts only. The Principles do not apply when the contract does not include a choice-of-law-clause. In addition, they are not a solution when the law chosen leads to an **annulment** ⚭ of the contract. In addition, they do not address the problems that can arise in the long-term. It is not clear what to do when the law chosen by the parties changes significantly in the course of legal reform.

In other areas, such as property law, torts, or family law disputes, issues of applicable law can also give rise to legal uncertainty. However, in family law, for instance, other HCCH instruments govern the choice, such as the Convention on the Law Applicable to Matrimonial Property Regimes, adopted in 1978, or the Hague Protocol on Law Applicable to Maintenance Obligations, adopted in 2007.

For EU member states, regulations Rome I and Rome II play a significant role in determining which applicable law is chosen. Rome I applies to contractual obligations in civil and commercial matters. It states both that party autonomy applies and that the parties can change the applicable law at any time if they agree. Rome I also clarifies that when no law has been selected, the case will be dealt with under the law of the country that is the primary residence of the main actor in the contract. It also entails rules applicable to specific contracts. Rome II, by contrast, applies to noncontractual obligations in civil and commercial matters. It deals with issues of liability, such as of products or the acts of another person. According to Rome II, the applicable law in most cases will be that of the country where the damage occurs. However, if the parties agree and under certain conditions, they are free to choose the applicable law. Overall, the effect of these two regulations is that no matter where in the EU a legal action is taken, the rules that determine the applicable law will be the same.

6. Recognition and Enforcement of Judgments

Judgments have to be enforced to be meaningful, of course. In cross-border disputes, this might mean that the judgment needs to be enforced abroad. The first step a court in the foreign country must take is to recognize the judgment. That is, the court of country A must accept the judicial decision of the court in country B, either through a unilateral act, or based on the *principle of comity*, under which states recognize and respect each other's judicial acts. The second step is enforcing the decision. The process of enforcement can differ from country to country, however. Courts may also have valid reasons to deny a foreign court's judgment, such as if the procedure is seen as unfair, or other rights of the parties have been violated, or doubt exists about the jurisdiction of the court that rendered the judgment.

The recent growth in cross-border disputes intensifies calls for clear rules on recognition and enforcement of foreign judgments. Nevertheless, the international community has found it quite difficult to agree until now. The Choice of Court Convention, mentioned in part 4, deals with recognition and enforcement of the judgment rendered by the court the parties have chosen. It is not applicable, however, when the parties do not select the court, such as in a tort case. The Hague Conference has also been working on the **Judgments Project**, the aim of which is to draft a new convention on the recognizing and enforcing judgments on civil or commercial matters, one that takes into account existing differences in national laws and promotes global circulation of judgments. In particular, the convention is also supposed to apply to and offer solutions for cases in which the disputing parties did not agree on a court to decide the case.

On a regional level, EU regulations and other instruments, such as the Lugano Convention, cover recognition and enforcement of judgments within the EU; the Lugano Convention extends to Iceland, Norway, and Switzerland. The Organization of American States has developed similar conventions covering the American continents.

International Family Law

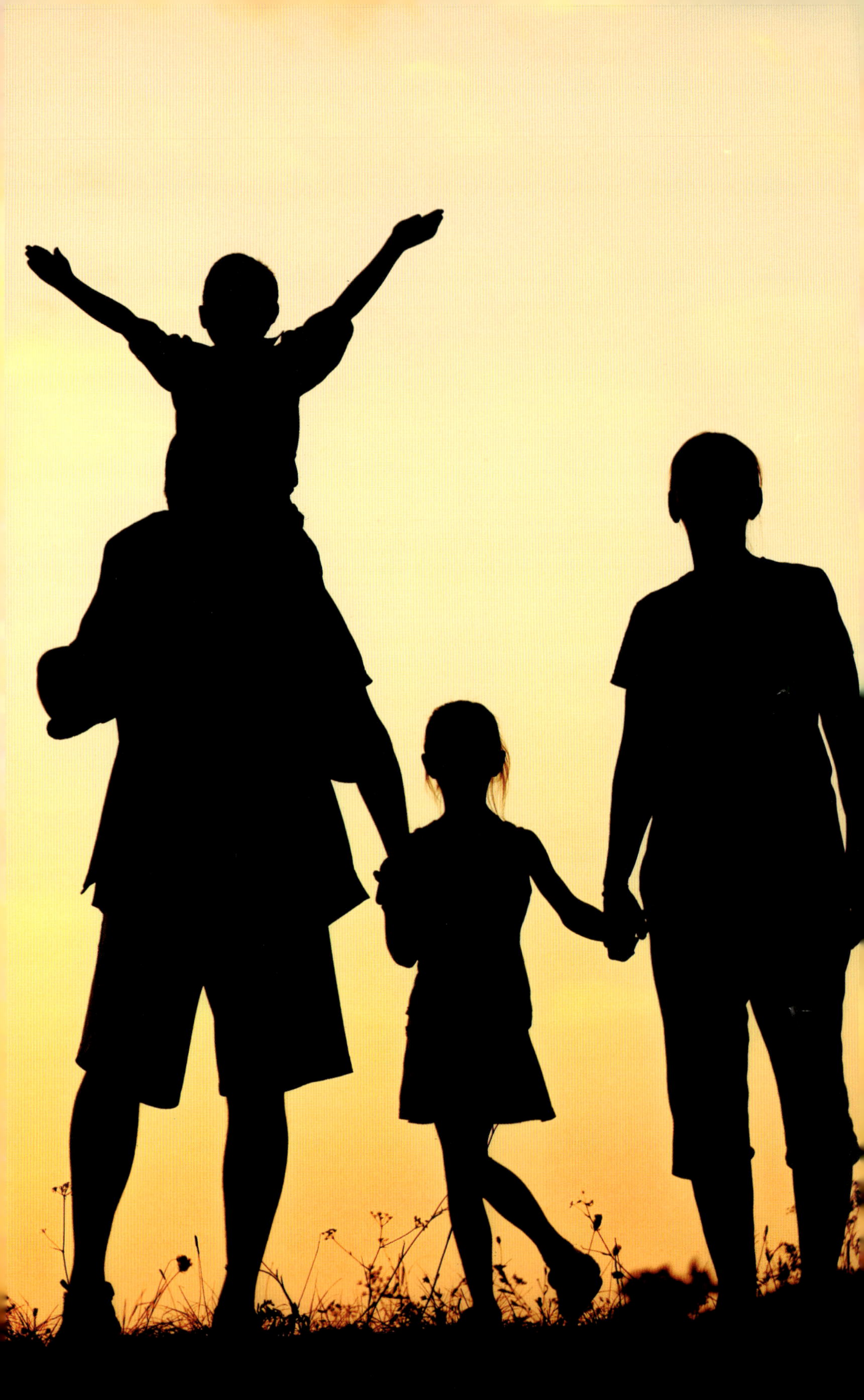

International Family Law 4

What to expect from this chapter?

This chapter provides an overview of current challenges in international family law, explaining in part 2 the development of family law efforts on the international level and presenting basic family rights in international human rights law. Part 3 addresses current challenges in child protection. Part 4 addresses intercountry adoption and international surrogacy arrangements. Part 5 is concerned with challenges in the field of international adult protection.

1. Introduction

Although most national laws recognize and protect a traditional family concept, that is to say: a group of people with 'common blood', today more and more other forms of family life are emerging that do not fit into the historic pattern, such as blended families, or families with two mothers or two fathers. In addition, a growth in cross-border movement of people increases relationships with an international dimension. These families may be involved in marriages, divorces, child support, or adoptions. International cases involve at least two jurisdictions, but because national family law systems differ from one country to another, international families do not always know which law is decisive and whether their relationship is recognized. To overcome this legal uncertainty ∽ and to facilitate the life of families, the international community has adopted rules of private international law ∽ aimed at answering three questions:

ture on page 79; The Merry Family, by Jan Steen, 1668.

(1) which court has jurisdiction, (2) which law is applicable, and (3) which circumstances determine whether a foreign decision is to be recognized in a local jurisdiction? These questions are dealt with in the chapter on Private International Law. The present chapter focuses more specifically on current family law issues, being a domain of international law with both private and public law characteristics.

2. The Development and Basis of International Family Law

The development of international family law standards started more than a century ago with the establishment of The *Hague Conference on Private International Law* (HCCH). Since its first meeting in 1893, the Conference has been concerned with legal issues related to family life. The agenda of the first session was in fact highly influenced by family law matters. Today, one of the organization's aim is still to improve the life of families, by increasing *legal security* and *certainty* in cross-border situations.

In 1993, the international family law community came together at the first *World Congress on Family Law and Children's Rights*. This congress takes place every four years. In 2013, representatives of governments, legal practitioners, politics, and civil society came together for the sixth time to discuss various topics and current trends related to family law. The next congress is planned for 2017. Issues such as domestic violence, international child relocation and placement, international enforcement of child support, or intercountry adoption were on the table, as well as the promotion of a network of international family law judges. Throughout the years, the congress constantly initiated action and reforms that directly or indirectly led to benefits for the protection of children and families worldwide. The International Society of Family Law (ISFL) has the same goal. Since its founding in 1973 in the United Kingdom, it developed into a society whose members include more than six hundred family law academics and legal practitioners. On a regular basis, it organizes world and regional conferences on current issues in family law.

Next to the efforts on the international level, international cooperation in the field of family law also takes place between the member states of the European Union. In fact, since the Treaty of Amsterdam entered into force ⌀ in 1999, a considerable amount of new regulations ⌀ that in one way or another deal with family law matters has been adopted by the EU. For example, the Brussels II-bis Regulation, in force since 2005, deals with divorce matters, the rights of children in proceedings, child abduction and protection, but also with the recognition and enforcement⌀ of decisions within the EU. The Rome III Regulation which is in force since 2012 aims at enhanced cooperation of EU Member states in the law applicable to divorce and legal separation. In the past 5 years, the European Commission has also been active in drafting legislation ⌀ that deals with matrimonial property law and property-related legal issues that arise after a couple separates which has not been married but instead living in a registered partnership for example.

p. 72

What do human rights treaties say?

Within the domain of public international law are several *international and regional human rights treaties* that include provisions relevant to family law issues. One is the *right to respect for private and family life*, which can be found in a number of treaties, such as the International Covenant on Economic, Social, and Cultural Rights (ICESCR), and also in the Universal Declaration of Human Rights (UDHR). In addition, the International Covenant on Civil and Political Rights (ICCPR) and the UDHR state that everyone has the *right to marry and to establish a family*. Another treaty proclaiming these rights is the Convention on the Elimination of All Forms of Discrimination against Women. The International Convention on the Protection of the Rights of All Migrant Workers and Members of Their Families explicitly deals with the protection and rights of families of migrant workers.

In addition, a number of children's rights, as stated in the UN Convention on the Rights of the Child (UNCRC), play a significant role for family law matters. The World Congress on Family Law and Children's Rights recently stressed the relevance of this convention for guidance on how to address family law matters and how to put them into practice. The principle of *the child's best interest*, for example, is considered one of the fundamental principles of international family law. It calls on all adults, whether in public or private function, to take all decisions affecting a child in the child's best interest.

Also regional human rights treaties touch upon the rights of families. The American Convention on Human Rights includes an article dedicated to the rights of the family. The same is true of the Arab Charter on Human Rights. In Europe, the European Convention on Human Rights and Fundamental Freedoms grants the right to respect for family life and the right to marry.

3. Challenges in International Child Protection

The best interest of the child principle has also influenced the drafting and implementation of international agreements in the area of child protection, which is one of the main areas of concern in international family law. The principle plays a significant role in, for instance, the *Hague Convention on the Civil Aspects of International Child Abduction*, which was adopted in 1980. This convention deals in particular with the risk of parental child abduction to several thousands of children each year. A child is being abducted when wrongfully removed or retained from his or her habitual residence, or not returned to his or her habitual residence. The removal is wrongful when the permission of one of the parents is missing. A common case is when one spouse of a mixed nationality couple takes the common child to his or her home country and never returns.

Resolving these kinds of cases requires international legal cooperation because more than one country's legal system is affected. Questions about jurisdiction and applicable law come up and resolving these challenges can take quite some time. The most important consideration, however, is always to protect the child. This is precisely the aim of the Hague Convention on the Civil Aspects of International Child Abduction. It sets out a framework for international cooperation to initiate the prompt return of abducted children. More specifically, the Convention states that the abducted child must be brought back to the country of his or her habitual residence as soon as possible. In this context, the habitual residence approach means that the respective authority must identify the place of ordinary residence of the child, which can be where the parent or parents live, or where he or she goes to school or kindergarten. International law does not provide for a strict definition of what habitual residence exactly entails but is used to acknowledge the best interest of the child. There can be only one habitual residence where the individual usually resides and routinely returns to after work or visiting other places. It is the geographical place considered home for a reasonably significant period.

The convention also acknowledges the best interest of the child in prescribing that any proceedings on abduction cases need to assess how long the child has lived in the other country and whether the child has become settled there. At the moment, ninety-three states have entered the agreement. States that have not entered the agreement have begun to adopt bilateral agreements with similar conditions.

CAUGHT ON CAMERA
DRAMATIC KIDNAPPING ATTEMPT
QUICK-THINKING SIBLINGS SAVE THE DAY

Other situations in transnational family relationships can also put children at risk. Examples include parental disputes over responsibility for or contact with the child, child support, or international relocation of the child. In many of these disputes, questions arise about who represents the child or how to protect a child's property. To support countries in protecting children who face such situations, in 1996 the HCCH adopted the *Convention on Jurisdiction, Applicable Law, Recognition, Enforcement and Co-operation in respect of Parental Responsibility and Measures for the Protection of Children* (also referred to as the *Convention on Parental Responsibility and Protection of Children*). It covers a wide range of procedural and substantive issues and supports countries in recognizing foreign legal measures of child protection. Thus it also helps the authorities in determining the court and the law to deal with a certain case.

The biggest challenge in international child protection today is handling cases where the Hague conventions and other international agreements do *not* apply. For instance, when a child who is being abducted is not habitually resident in a country party to the abduction convention, the effect of the convention is quite limited. Such cases are then typically addressed through diplomatic channels. In general, however, there is much effort for cooperation also between countries not party to any of the conventions mentioned. In 2004, for example, the HCCH created the so-called Malta-Process, which established a dialogue between legal experts and judges of states that are parties to the conventions and states that are not and whose legal system is based on or influenced by sharia. To further strengthen the communication with countries that have an Islamic legal background, the city of The Hague hosted an international seminar titled "Islamic Legal Perspectives on Cross-Border Family Disputes Involving Children" in 2014. The same year, the International Child Abduction Center of the Netherlands (Centre IKO) hosted a conference in the Peace Palace for family lawyers who work in the field of in international parental child abduction.

4. About Inter-Country Adoption and Surrogacy Arrangements

International standards on child protection are also important in intercountry or international adoptions. Inter-country adoption relates to the adoption and actual move of a child from one country to another. What happens in this agreement is a transfer of parental rights, from either the biological parents or the current guardians to the adopting parents. In the international case, more than one national legal system is inevitably involved in the procedure. Both words – 'inter-country' and 'international' – are often used through one another. International adoption first became a phenomenon after World War II, and was intended to help orphaned children in Europe. Over the years, the number of international adoptions rose and the lack of standards led to the adoption of the *Hague Convention on Protection of Children and Co-operation in Respect of Intercountry Adoption (Hague Adoption Convention)* in May 1993.

The goal of the convention is to establish security, predictability, and transparency for all parties involved in the adoption process and to respect the fundamental rights of the child. To achieve these goals, the convention facilitates cooperation between the contracting states via national central authorities.

With its ninety-six state parties, as of June 2016, the Convention has a considerable reach. In introducing several standards and principles, it has made a significant contribution to regulating intercountry adoptions. For example, the Convention states that before any adoption can take place, the authorities must be sure that all possibilities for the child being raised by its birth family or the extended family have been exhausted. It also clarifies that the official adoption process can in fact happen before or after the child is moved to the home country or country of residence of the future parents. Further, the Convention stipulates that international adoption should only be an option if national solutions are not adequate. This is called the *subsidiarity principle* and is designed to protect birth families from exploitation.

In August 2014, the International Institute of Social Studies in The Hague hosted the *International Forum on Intercountry Adoption and Global Surrogacy*, which acknowledged that international adoption is still a debated issue. The Forum also realized that legal issues and disputes connected to intercountry adoption are decreasing, which is related to the fact that adoption numbers are dropping overall. By way of illustration, in 2009, the Netherlands counted 682 international adoptions; in 2014, this number decreased to 354 (www.adoptie.nl). This decrease may be related to the newest developments in reproductive technology that enhance a woman's ability to have her own biological children even if she cannot be pregnant. For instance, cases of international surrogacy were increasing in the past decade. Surrogacy refers to an arrangement between a couple or a single person and a woman, often in form of a contract about the woman's carrying and giving birth to a child for the couple or person. International surrogacy arrangements usually result in the birth of a child by a surrogate mother in one country with genetic or intended parents from another country. The current global trend of surrogacy is again the result of advanced technology and medical science, as well as facilitated international mobility.

One prominent international surrogacy case that made news headlines worldwide in 2014 is that of Baby Gammy. A Thai woman entered into a surrogacy arrangement with an Australian couple. After she gave birth to twins, the Australian couple took only the girl back with them to Australia, leaving the boy, who suffers from Down syndrome, behind. Shortly after this story became public, debates broke out about the duties and rights of the couple and the surrogate mother and about status and recognition of the surrogacy contract.

What legal problems are related to international surrogacy arrangements?

The debates on the Baby Gammy case reflect the numerous legal problems that surround international surrogacy arrangements, mainly because surrogacy arrangements touch upon moral issues that are approached differently in various states. Indeed, the arrangements involve nationals from multiple countries. In some cases, the eggs of the surrogate mother and the sperm of the intended father are used, and these two biological parents might not even have the same nationality. In other cases, foreign egg or sperm donors are used, sometimes both. In most cases, the surrogate mother is carrying a child to whom she is not genetically related. Then, the state where the pregnant woman lives or the agreement is closed may differ from the state in which the child is born or will be raised.

In some countries surrogacy arrangements are illegal (for example Finland, Pakistan and most Islamic countries), while in other countries surrogacy is unregulated, meaning neither prohibition nor permission (Ireland for example). Yet other countries allow surrogacy and even regulate commercial or for-profit surrogacy (for example India).

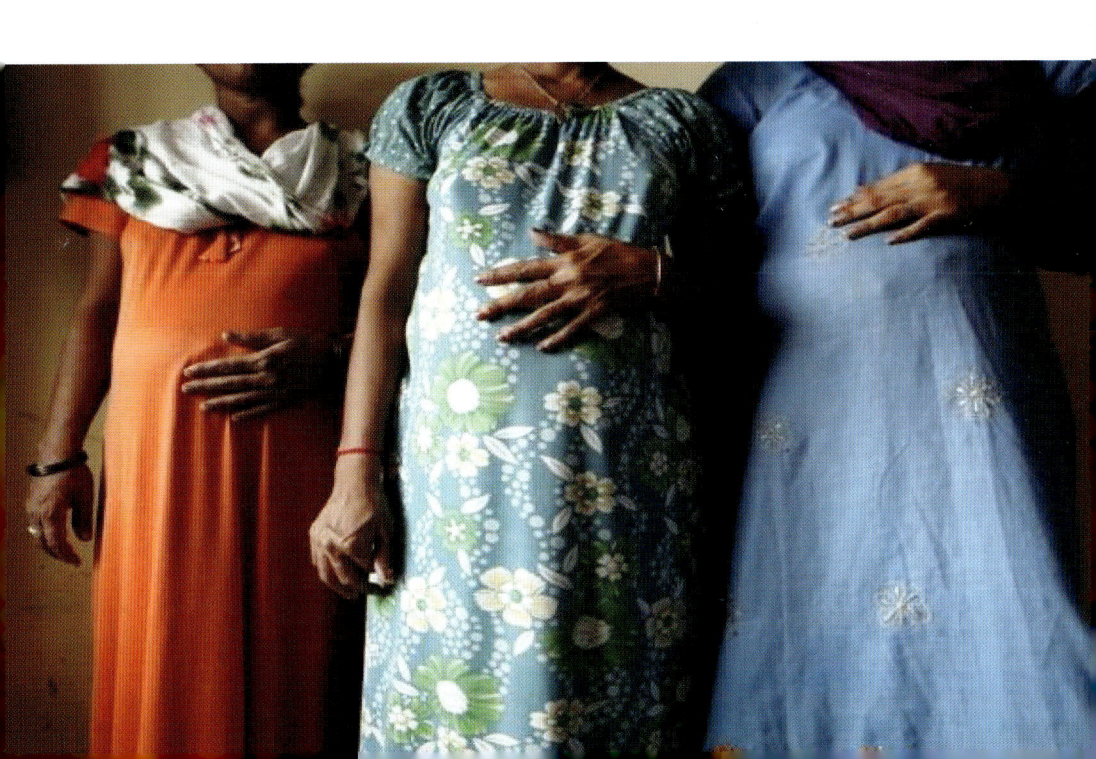

Surrogate mothers often come from a poor background and are pressured into surrogate arrangements for the economic benefit that the mother and her family will gain. In fact, the divide between sending and receiving countries resembles the divide between developed and developing countries, the divide between rich and poor. Intended parents often face misinformation with regard to the legal difficulties that await them, as well as to the costs involved, which vary greatly depending on the countries involved. These circumstances make it clear that surrogacy is not a transparent business and cases of illegal, premature, and ill-prepared surrogacy arrangements are in fact numerous.

Human rights concerns relate to both the practice of surrogacy as such and the consequences to the surrogate mother and the child. Human rights law gives the child the right to a nationality and to know its identity. Ethical considerations about "trade in children" and "renting of body parts" are also prevalent, as are concerns about the psychological and physical health risks for both mother and child. All these concerns have to be dealt with, but because surrogacy is a new trend and technical and medical innovation often moves more quickly than law, the international standards to deal with these concerns still need to be created. Although the Hague Adoption Convention has been referred to in surrogacy cases, the HCCH Special Commission on Surrogacy rejected it as an appropriate instrument.

5. Challenges in International Adult Protection

International family law is concerned with the protection of not only children but also adults. More specifically, it is concerned with laws of international marriage and international divorce. Divorce as such already has great potential for dispute, but the international cases in particular bring considerable challenges to national and international family law. For instance, a couple who lives in a country other than their home country or country they were married and then decides to divorce is likely to be confronted with numerous administrative and legal obstacles. Again, more than one country's laws are involved and the question arises as to which court in which country has jurisdiction over the case. If the laws on divorce were the same in all countries, no problems would present themselves. The reality is that legal systems differ from one country to another and which law applies in a particular set of circumstances needs to be determined. In many cases, one jurisdiction might favor one party and disfavor the other. This often leads to what is called *forum-shopping*, the practice of "shopping" for the legal system (forum) that is most convenient and favorable to the parties. Even after the legal forum and jurisdiction have been established, other obstacles might arise. The mere fact that one country accepted a divorce does not necessarily mean that other countries will also recognize it.

With regard to international marriages, several developments in family law currently challenge related national and international laws. For one, some countries recently witnessed an increase in the number of *bogus marriage*, also called 'fraud marriage' or 'marriage of convenience'. In many cases, the aim of such marriages is for one party to gain a residence permit in a new country. Non-EU nationals, for example, gain a residence permit when they marry an EU national.

In connection to marriage and divorce, international family law is also concerned with laws on equal treatment of women. For example, not everywhere do women have the same position in matters of divorce as men. Furthermore, in many countries the custody is automatically considered to be a matter of the mother only, instead of being a matter of both, mother and father.

Recently, the increasing possibilities for same-sex partnerships to formalize their relationships challenge international and national law. At the moment, differences across countries are considerable. Some grant same-sex couples the right to marry (Belgium, the Netherlands, the United States, France and Spain, for instance); other countries offer a formal registration of a same-sex partnership as *civil partnership*, also referred to as registered partnership or civil union (Denmark or Sweden, for instance); and yet other countries give certain benefits to same-sex couples, such as tax exemptions (Argentina and some states of the United States, for instance) and new forms of parenthood, such as co-motherhood for lesbian couples. The latter is the case in for example The Netherlands.

It is one thing to formalize these relationships, it is yet another to recognize them internationally. Although certain countries might grant a same-sex couple the status of a registered partnership or the right to marry, other countries do not. What happens if a same-sex couple who marry in country A then move to country B, which does not recognize their marriage, and then want to divorce? Can country B refuse to deal with the divorce? In addition, in other areas registered or married same-sex couples do not enjoy the same rights – such as parenting – as opposite-sex couples. Although changes are underway, many countries continue to criminalize same-sex marriages and partnerships.

What does international law say on same-sex couples?

International human rights standards on the right to marry apply to everyone. The ongoing problem is that a number of treaties and other documents refer to marriage using the words *men* and *women*. One international treaty that keeps marriage gender-neutral is the Hague Convention on Celebration and Recognition of the Validity or Marriages from 1978, which, however, only three states have signed. In 2007, the International Commission on Civil Status adopted the *Convention on the Recognition of Registered Partnerships,* the first international treaty to mention same-sex partnerships explicitly. Other human rights treaties that apply to this issue are those prohibiting discrimination on grounds of sex or other status. The trend in international case law is that sexual orientation discrimination is forbidden, specifically that states may not discriminate between unmarried same-sex couples and unmarried different-sex couples. Hence, international law tends toward more protection of same-sex couples and entails standards that promote a stronger protection, but many countries do not accept international standards and deal with family law exclusively on a national level.

The United Nations Office at Geneva, Palais des Nations.

International Economic Law

The G-20 meeting in Turkey, 20

International Economic Law 5

What to expect from this chapter?

This chapter first provides an overview of global economic law that covers legal developments in international trade. In part 3, it explains the development of international law in relation to finance and investment matters. Part 4 goes on to address legal trends in international sales and contracts. The final part discusses the connection between global economic law and development.

1. Introduction

Globalization makes it considerably easier for individuals and for companies to enter into transnational economic relations. Today, for example, buying goods and services from abroad is commonplace. International economic law is concerned with far more than private international commercial relations, however. It in fact covers all kinds of international economic encounters between all kinds of actors, including states, international organizations ∞, and companies. More specifically, it is about legal and institutional regulation of trade (in goods and services), investment, finance, intellectual property, sales, contracts, and many other issues. In an increasingly interconnected world, more of these interdependent aspects come up constantly. The biggest challenge is to remain flexible, to adapt to new economic trends, and to meet new needs. Development is just one of the many issues that international economic law addresses.

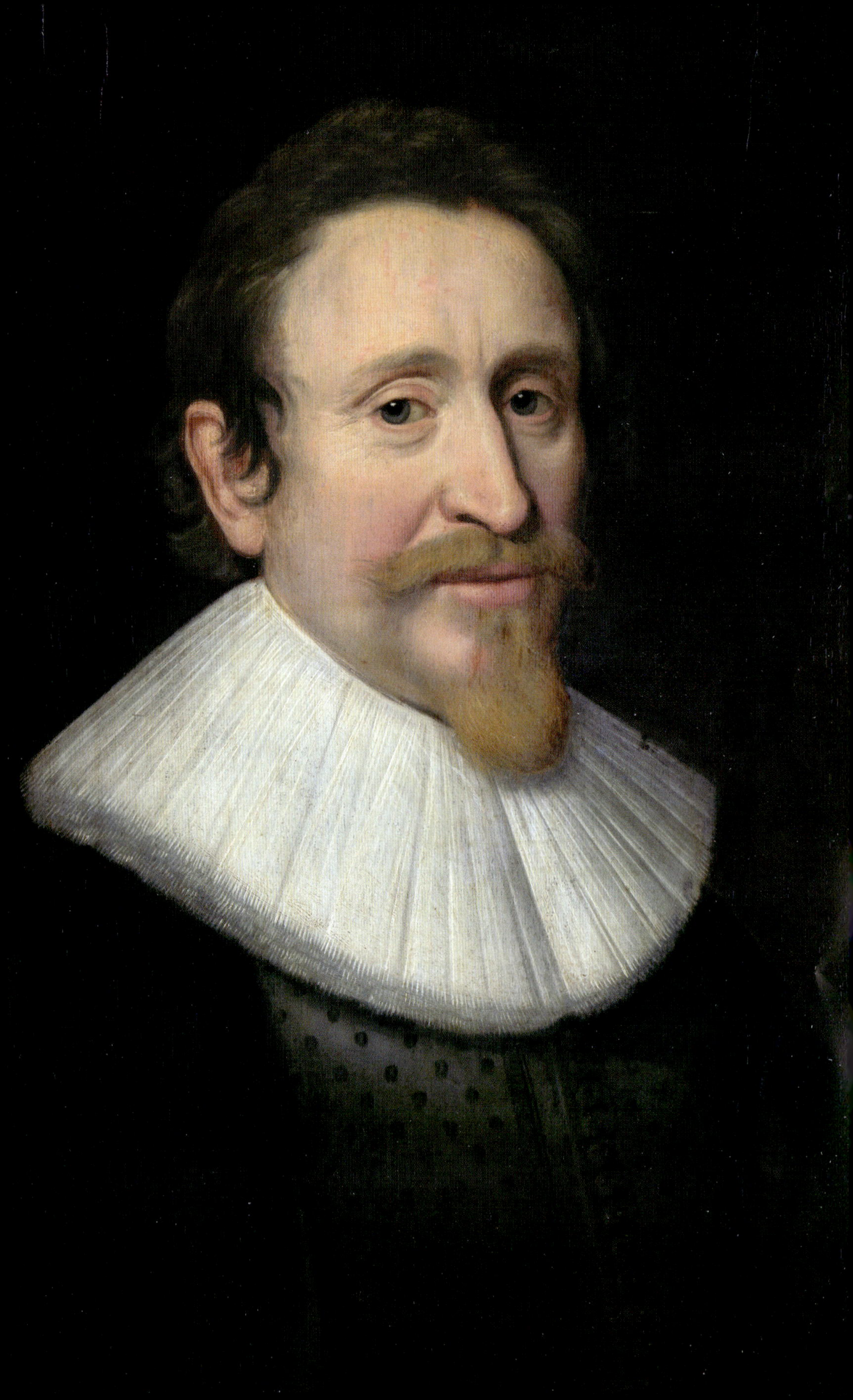

About Hugo Grotius
(born 10 April 1583 in Delft and died 28 August 1645 in Rostock)
... and how a box full of books saved his life:

At the age of fifteen, Hugo Grotius took part in his first diplomatic mission to France, where he then began to study law. On finishing his studies, he returned to the Netherlands and started working as a lawyer. After more than a decade as a successful jurist, Grotius was imprisoned on a religious charge in 1619 and sentenced by a special tribunal to life imprisonment. While imprisoned, he was allowed to receive packages, typically filled with books and essays, to keep him up to date. It was in one of these boxes that Grotius managed to escape to Paris in 1621, where he then lived for more than a decade. In 1634, Grotius moved to Sweden and was appointed ambassador to France. Ten years later, Queen Christina asked Grotius to return to Sweden to take up a new position. Not long after, however, Grotius died in a shipwreck.

Why is Grotius important to international law?

Between 1604 and 1605, Grotius wrote his first book, *De Jure Praedae Commentarius (Treatise on the Law of Prize)*, though as a whole it was never published. Only the chapter "De Mare Liberum" was released and it had a great influence on the development of the law of the sea. Grotius believed that the seas belong to no country but are open to all, a concept that became the legal basis for the Dutch efforts to conquer Portuguese possessions and to participate in the East Indian trade. Grotius was active in other fields of international law and relations as well. In 1615, he published a document listing the conditions under which Jews fleeing the Inquisition could settle in the Netherlands. His subsequent imprisonment did not end his contributions to international law. After his escape to Paris, he finished *De Jure Belli Ac Pacis*, a book on the law of war and peace. In it, he asserted that waging war is unlawful except under certain circumstances – foresight into the international legal order of the twenty-first century. It was this book that earned Grotius the title of father of international law.

2. Fundamentals of Global Economic Law

For most of history, international economic activities were almost exclusively related to trade. The famous 1609 publication by *Hugo Grotius* on the freedom of the high seas was commissioned by the Dutch East Indies Company expressly to make international trade, with Asia in particular, easier.

Global economic law in Grotius' day and until the twentieth century was a decentralized system of different national rules on trade relations between states. The lesson of the two world wars, however, was that countries realized they each needed to rebuild their destroyed cities and territories as quickly as possible. To speed up economic recovery, cooperation was essential: no country is better off on its own. Gradually also support for and the benefits of a more universal and harmonized global economy became apparent.

Today, the biggest component of global economic law is trade law. In 1947, twenty-three countries signed the *General Agreement on Tariffs and Trade* (GATT) *in Geneva* to make trading among them easier. In the years that followed, international trade relations developed rapidly and the number of countries wanting to join the agreement grew. Over the course several rounds of multilateral trade negotiations, each named after the country where the round was launched, the GATT evolved into a worldwide organization. In 1995, as a result of the 'Uruguay Round', the GATT was renamed the *World Trade Organization* (WTO). Currently, the WTO counts 160 member states. Its main tasks are the regulation of international trade to facilitate worldwide import and export of goods and services for all its members, and to make trade flow as freely as possible between them. On a regular base, member states meet to discuss and agree on common principles that form the basis of international trade law.

What are the common principles of international trade?

The principle of most favored nation (MFN) – also referred to as the principle of nondiscrimination – is one of the fundamental principles of the WTO. It requires member states to treat other member states equally and not to discriminate between trading partners. The principles of reciprocity, transparency, and fair competition are also central. Reciprocity refers to mutual changes in tariffs that the member states agree to. Transparency ensures that WTO members share their trade regulations and other trade-related decisions with each other. All WTO rules follow the principle of fair competition, which establishes what are fair and what are unfair trade practices.

Together with the principle of free trade, which bans national import or export restrictions, these four principles lay out the foundation of the WTO trading system. In particular, the principle of free trade has increasingly been challenged, for a long time, by representatives of civil society and states, in particular developing states, and today in response to the global economic crisis. Opponents criticize the difficulties this principle poses both for introducing standards to protect the environment and for developing countries to compete in a free trade environment. More and more countries turn to a protectionist policy that limits trade. WTO principles and rules, however, are in fact designed to make that difficult. Nevertheless, once the crisis began to unfold, different countries began to engage in trade-restrictive actions, such as increasing tariffs or license requirements for imports, with the aim of supporting national and local companies and countering domestic unemployment.

The WTO works with a number of committees and commissions to ensure that all member states follow the principles and rules. If a member state still feels that other states do not play by the rules, it can bring the case to the WTO's Dispute Settlement Body (DSB), which offers specific procedures for solving disputes.

One recent case dealt with by the DSB is European Communities – Measures Prohibiting the Importation and Marketing of Seal Products. In 2009, the European Community adopted a regulation banning the import of seal products because of concerns over the cruel ways of killing these animals. The regulation did not apply to seal products from indigenous communities. Canada and Norway claimed that the ban and the exceptions were thus not in agreement with WTO rules in that they discriminated against some member states. After some consultations, the DSB Panel in 2013 found that the ban as such is not contrary to WTO rules, but that the exceptions included in the regulation indeed discriminate. It therefore required the EU to change the regulation. The case triggered considerable public attention in being one of the first to deal with trade and animal welfare concerns. For some people, the outcome of the case is also critical because it can be interpreted as assigning WTO principles more weight than moral values on animal protection.

In addition to goods, the WTO is also concerned with services and intellectual property. The *Agreement on Trade-Related Aspects of Intellectual Property Rights* (TRIPS), adopted in 1994, divides the protection of intellectual property rights into two areas: copyrights for mainly artistic work, and *patents* for distinctive signs on goods and industrial property. Patents protect the innovative ideas of their creators and are especially important for engineers and the pharma industry. In recent years, some controversy has revolved around how the TRIPS applies to pharmaceuticals, given loopholes in the agreement that allow someone other than the original manufacturer to produce a patented drug, exclusively for the domestic market (*compulsory licensing*). As a result, the original manufacturer receives (much) less revenues from the drug involved and a number of these licenses could undermine the purpose of patents. At the other end, compulsory licensing makes it possible for developing countries to gain access to legal drugs they otherwise could not afford, such as HIV/AIDs medication. Since India issued one of these compulsory licenses in 2012, concerns have mounted as to how some of these licenses might actually discriminate against the patent owner and eventually undermine the purpose of patents.

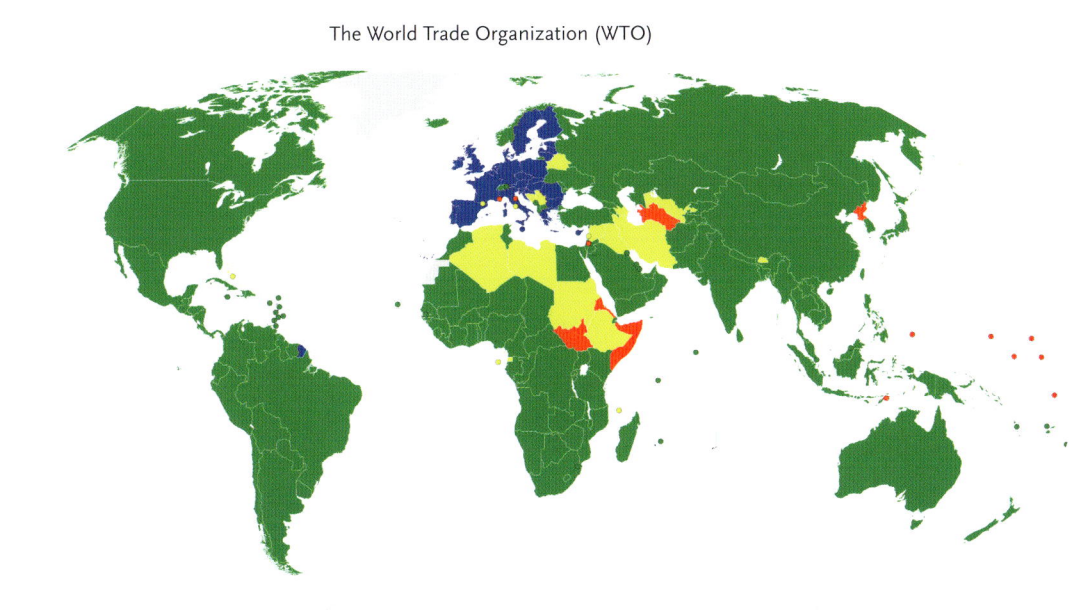

The World Trade Organization (WTO)

Members | Members, dually represented by the EU | Observers | Non-participant states

Various international and regional organizations are active in the field of patent protection. The *European Patent Office* (EPO), based in The Hague, is responsible for giving out patents for not only European but also worldwide innovations. It is the executive arm of the European Patent Organization, a financially and politically independent nongovernmental entity. Every day, the EPO searches for and examines European and international patent applications from individual inventors or companies. The decision to grant a patent is usually taken by a team of three. The office also deals with oppositions filed against granted patents. In 2013, the EPO considered more than 260,000 filings. Currently, it holds a collection of more than seventy million patent documents that are available online. In June 2014, construction began for the new EPO building in The Hague.

Did you know that ...

at the European Patent Office some 65 percent of European patent applications are filed by non-European companies, mostly from the United States, Japan, China, and South Korea?

Established:	1977 by the European Patent Convention (EPC) of 1973
Main activities:	Grants patents under the EPC and promotes innovation and economic growth in Europe and worldwide
Structure:	Office and Administrative Council
Members:	9 members, 3 members appointed by each Government and 3 (third-country) members selected by the 6 government-appointed members
Official language:	English, French and German
Website:	http://www.epo.org/

3. International Finance and Investment Law

After World War II, the initiatives in international trade cooperation also triggered developments in international financial and monetary cooperation. In July 1944, 44 states came together at a conference in the United States to deliberate the rebuilding of the international economic system. One of the outcomes of this conference, known as Bretton Woods for its location, was the establishment of the *International Monetary Fund* (IMF). Charged with addressing the monetary challenges that arose out of the expanding international trade, the IMF today is responsible more broadly for promoting economic growth and stability through enabling international monetary cooperation and exchange rate stability. It comprises 188 states parties, to whom it gives policy and technical advice. It also gives financial support to individual states in case of serious balance of payment problems, so as to prevent these problems from affecting other countries and eventually the world economy. When the global financial crisis hit in 2008, the IMF played an essential role in granting loans to member states to help them face the situation. The IMF was for instance

Bretton Woods meeting 1944.

active in helping out Greece, after the then newly elected government in 2009 revealed the truth about the country's public deficit. After a massive bailout plan, the IMF worked with various soft law instruments, such as stand-by agreements or letters of intent, to restore market confidence and fiscal sustainability in Greece.

In addition to the IMF, the Group of Seven (G7) emerged in practice as a leading forum for consultation on financial and monetary policies. This group consists of the seven leading industrial states: the United States, Japan, Germany, United Kingdom, France, Italy, and Canada. For a while the G7 was extended to the G8, to include Russia. Also, the G20, which is made up of the finance ministers and central bank governors of nineteen countries and the EU, played a leading role in handling and mitigating the effects of the 2008 crisis. Among mostly economically advanced countries, the G20 also includes emerging economies, especially the BRICS countries (Brazil, Russia, India, China, and South Africa). In 1999, the G20 met for the first time to discuss current economic and monetary global challenges. Since then, the group has met annually to find ways to optimize international financial regulation and institutions.

The BRICS leaders in 2014

What about international investment law?

In response to the global financial crisis, to better control the negative effects of the crisis on their national economies, states began to turn away from open economy policies. This move led to a rise in protectionism, also fed by a growth in foreign investment, and over the past years, approximately three thousand bilateral and regional investment treaties have been concluded. These are primarily agreements on the terms of private investment by a company or individual in one state investing in a project in another state. The purpose of these treaties is primarily to protect the foreign investor in the host country and to promote foreign investment by maximizing trust and minimizing the risk of the foreign investor. Together with national law and international law on foreign investment, the agreements make up international investment law.

Along with these developments came international investment disputes. Most investment treaties include rules that in the event of a legal dispute on the investment the parties must turn to arbitration. The Permanent Court of Arbitration (PCA) and the International Centre for the Settlement of Investment Disputes (ICSID) both deal with investment disputes regularly.

p. 49

> *One recent case dealt with by the ICSID concerns the Swedish power company Vattenfall and the government of Germany. Their dispute related to new environmental restrictions by the German government that, according to the claimant, stand in the way of Vattenfall's investments in German nuclear power plants. The first arbitration proceedings lasted from 2009 until 2011. In 2012, Vattenfall filed new proceedings against Germany before the ICSID. Germany held that German and EU law on environmental protection required the restrictions. Vattenfall asserted that the restrictions were an emotional response to the Japanese nuclear power plant disaster following the 2011 tsunami, that the restrictions breach the investment contract and prevent Vattenfall from gaining revenues from their investment. The case, which is still pending, exemplifies the difficulty of balancing public state interests and private economic interests of a company.*

The draft Transatlantic Trade and Investment Partnership (TTIP) between the EU and the United States also entails a clause allowing companies to file cases against governments before an international arbitral tribunal to protect their investment. This might cause states to turn to protectionist measures in their foreign investment policies. In fact, a number of countries recently have begun to apply more restrictive language to their investment treaties, both to avoid broad interpretations of the provisions and to limit the power of the investing party. If such practices pile up in the future, foreign investments will stall, which could have a negative effect on international cooperation in investment matters, but potentially also on the overall international economic cooperation.

4. International Law of Sales and Contracts

Another branch of global economic law is international commercial law, which is basically made up of private international law rules on sales and contracts. In 1980, eighteen countries signed the *UN Convention on Contracts for the International Sale of Goods*, which was established by the *UN Commission on International Trade Law* (UNCITRAL) and is the main multilateral treaty in this domain. Relevant private international law rules are also shaped by The Hague Conference on Private International Law (HCCH). From the start, the HCCH has been concerned with international commercial law, in particular that relating to contracts, trusts, security claims, and foreign companies. In regular meetings, member states negotiate and draft multilateral treaties on a long list of issues of which commercial law is only one. The Conference also closely cooperates with UNCITRAL.

p. 69

In general, international commercial law deals with commercial transactions and agreements for that purpose between parties from different countries. Globalization and other developments in technology make such transactions more numerous and more complex. For example, many today's international commercial transactions take place online. These types of transactions challenge both national and international law to find solutions for the countless variety of new situations and disputes that arise because of this new marketplace. The revival of *lex mercatoria* (Latin for merchant law), a legal system dating to the Middle Ages, is one way of addressing some of these challenges. *Lex mercatoria* is a body of legal principles developed by merchants active in international trade, to resolve international commercial disputes outside of courts. Examples include nondiscrimination between merchants from different countries and the obligation of good faith. It is based on unwritten law, commercial customs, and norms, but recently has also been embodied in international agreements, such as the *UN Convention on Contracts for the International Sale of Goods*. Moreover, some courts regard *lex mercatoria* as an autonomous legal order and refer to it in arbitration proceedings. Others, though, still hesitate to use it as a source for resolving disputes because it is inconsistent, lacks universal definition, and is not broadly accepted.

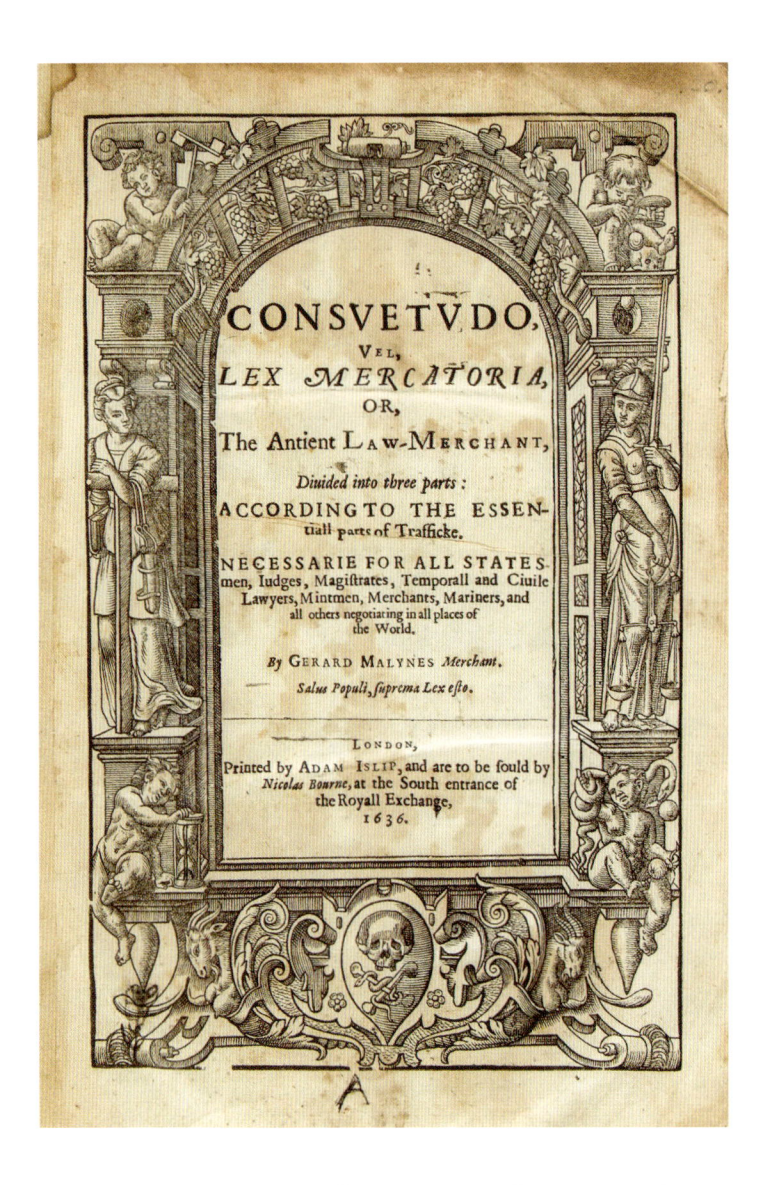

The increase in transnational operations of commercial entities not only challenges substantive law ↫, but also requires new procedural ↫ regulations. One example is choice of law ↫ in international contracts. If more than one legal system is involved in transnational economic actions, a decision needs to be taken as to which law governs the contract. It is common practice today for parties themselves to choose the law to be applied for the enforcement of their contract. This is the result of work done by the HCCH, among other institutions. In particular, the HCCH in recent years has been actively developing principles that can guide the choice of law in international commercial contracts. The *International Institute for the Unification of Private Law* (UNIDROIT) has also undertaken considerable work in the area of commercial law and harmonizing standards, especially with regard to contracts.

5. International Economy and Development

From the beginning, the global economic system has been strongly influenced by countries with advanced economic powers, making it difficult for developing countries and their economies to keep up. Because of their constant struggle for more influence on relevant policies and for regulations they could profit from, in the 1960s and the 1970s developing countries pushed for a *New International Economic Order* (NIEO). One of the most important aspects of this movement was the objective to stop former colonial powers from benefitting from the exploitation of the natural resources of colonial territories. In 1962, the UN General Assembly adopted a *Declaration on the Permanent Sovereignty over Natural Resources*. The political claim for economic development gradually evolved into a principle under international law, namely, the duty to cooperate in development through economic and social channels. This notion continues to play a significant role in developing countries and in debates on foreign investment regulation, environmental and sustainable development regulations, and concerns over scarcity of natural resources.

The Declaration was followed by various proposals on a new international economic order, first introduced at the UN Conference on Trade and Development (UNCTAD) in 1964. But even though a declaration to establish a NIEO and a Charter of Economic Rights and Duties were adopted by the UN General Assembly in 1974, only a few of the initiatives had a lasting impact. Nevertheless, the discussions have lead to greater attention by the international community on the interdependence of economic and development concerns. The *United Nations Millennium Declaration* is a good example in this regard. It includs eight Millennium Development Goals, among other things on eliminating poverty, promoting education and equality, and improving health standards worldwide. In September 2015, the Millennium Development Goals have been replaced by a new set of seventeen Sustainable Development Goals, which outline no fewer than 169 concrete targets, to be met within the next fifteen years.

What do the World Bank and WTO have to do with development?

International organizations are also concerned with the connection between economic issues and development. The leading organization in that arena is the World Bank, which together with the IMF, was established in 1944 at the Bretton Woods Conference. The initial purpose of the institution was to assist in the reconstruction of certain territories devastated by World War II, and to promote the development of already independent developing countries (particularly in Latin America) by providing capital through investments. The World Bank officially consists of the International Bank for Reconstruction and Development (IBRD) and the International Development Association (IDA). Collectively, the World Bank, the International Finance Corporation, the Multilateral Investment Guarantee Agency, and the ICSID make up the *World Bank Group*.

The World Bank office in Washington D.C., USA.

Today, the World Bank supports developing economies in combatting poverty and realizing shared prosperity. To achieve these goals, it provides low-interest loans or interest-free credits and grants for projects related to infrastructure improvement, environmental protection, or sustainability. The World Bank is also said to be the world's largest external funder of education activities. Currently, the World Bank Group uses its resources, which consist of member state contributions, to subsidize almost 1,800 projects in 109 countries. One remarkable aspect about the organization is its *Inspection Panel*, which was established in 1993. The panel gives amongst others individual citizens the opportunity to file a complaint if they are negatively affected by a World Bank project. In this way, the Panel functions as a quasi-judicial ☞ reviewer of projects that improves the overall accountability ☞ and legitimacy ☞ of the organization's work.

The WTO recognizes the link between economy and development, made clear by the inclusion in most WTO agreements of rules with special or differential treatment for developing countries. Developed countries may treat developing and least-developed countries more favorably than other WTO members with regard to the time allowed to implement an agreement.

International Law and Technology

PASSWORD
LOGIN

International Law and Technology 6

What to expect from this chapter?

The digital revolution demonstrates how technological developments can challenge the law. The goal of this chapter is to provide a sense of how international law responds to current trends and developments related to this transformation. It begins with the problem of cybercrime and how international law can help regulate the fight against it. Part 3 covers issues related to privacy rights and data protection. Part 4 addresses the challenges to intellectual property that come with the information society. Part 5 explores the issue of liability and the Internet in connection with free speech, intermediaries, and e-commerce.

1. Introduction

Technological developments constantly bring changes to society, whether in information technology, e-commerce, data protection, biotechnology, or medical science. The problem in all these fields is that technological developments move quickly and legal answers take time. In addition, ongoing globalization makes it easier for technological developments to cross borders, which makes it difficult for national legal systems to address related legal issues. Numerous initiatives have in recent decades therefore been undertaken to protect actors whose interests are at stake, such as consumers and other individuals, governments, or companies.

2. The Increasing Threat of Cybercrime

Worldwide, close to three billion people use the Internet today. Many of them will agree that the threat of becoming a victim of cybercrime has increased enormously in the last ten years. Many of them have in fact already become victims. Reports on attacks on websites, spamming or hacking of email accounts became regular components of our newscast. Per definition, a cybercrime can be any attack with computer hardware or software. But also online financial crimes such as payment card fraud or e-banking crimes are widespread and often occur in connection with identity theft. In addition, recent years have seen an increase in online sexual offenses, which is also related to mainstream use of social media. Children can be particularly affected by cybercrime, given that increased use of the Internet has made access to and distribution of child abuse material easier and more widespread. In the past, primarily individuals or small groups committed cybercrimes but today cybercriminal networks are common, and the underground market for various illegal activities is thriving.

What are the challenges in combating cybercrime?

The primary problem is that most cybercrime cases go undetected, either because victims are not aware that they are a victim, or because reporting mechanisms are not in place. Prosecuting cybercrime is also difficult in many cases because often more than one country is affected. One of the biggest challenges in prosecution is that not all countries outlaw and criminalize the same offenses. Criminals are aware of this weakness in the law and therefore choose to operate from countries where a particular act is not (yet) forbidden. Another challenge is that it is often not clear which state has the jurisdiction to prosecute. In most cases, such conflicts are resolved through either informal or formal negotiations between states. Nonetheless, differences in national legal systems make it difficult to combat cybercrime. Therefore, in recent decades, efforts for an international and regional approach to combat cybercrime have multiplied.

One of the more significant challenges for international, regional, and national law today is the investigation of cybercrimes. The first step is to identify who is responsible. Cybercriminals, however, find new ways to protect their identities every day, such as by operating in what are called *Darknet* sites and using anonymization networks such as Tor or providers that do not cooperate with law enforcement, known as bullet-proof providers. Such tools make those who use them relatively anonymous and difficult to trace. Darknet sites are hidden and not accessible via standard Internet browsers, but instead through a specific browser and networks designed to enable access, which are freely available for download. A collection of Darknet sites is referred to as Deep Web. Investigating such networks requires considerable international cooperation. In 2013, Silk Road, an online anonymous black market for illegal drugs and other equally illegal products, has been taken down by joint efforts of the United States' Federal Bureau of Investigation and Europol.

p. 38

What actions are taken on the international and regional level to fight cybercrime?

In early 2014, the Council of Europe launched a project called Cybercrime@Octopus, which aims to help countries around the world implement the 2001 Budapest Convention on Cybercrime, the main international treaty dealing with crimes committed online or within other computer networks. It specifically addresses crimes against the confidentiality, integrity, or availability of computers or data, but also other computer-related fraud and forgery, child pornography, and related copyright crimes. Furthermore, it brings in line all investigation powers and provides a framework for mutual legal assistance. Although it has been adopted by the Council of Europe, it is also open to countries that are not members of the Council of Europe. In fact, it has been ratified by countries worldwide, making it a successful international effort in harmonizing cybercrime law and facilitating cooperation. Within this project, the Council of Europe also organizes annual Octopus Conferences in Strasbourg, where government officials, Internet specialists, police officers, and other stakeholders meet to discuss and find solutions for today's challenges in cybercrime. In April 2015 the fourth Global Conference on Cyberspace took place in The Hague, where potential national and international responses to the threat of cybercrime, and general issues in relation to Internet governance were being discussed.

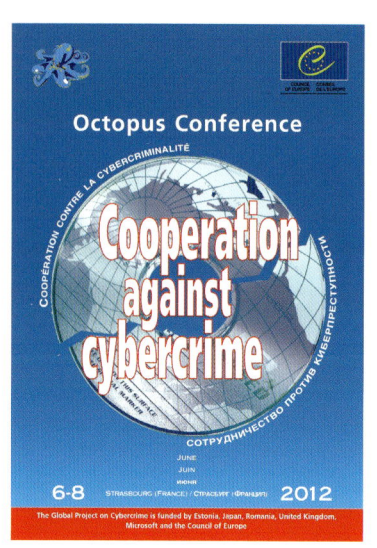

On an international level, Interpol is probably the best-known organization actively exchanging information and raising awareness about cybercrime. Its goal is to harmonize stakeholder efforts in the fight against cybercrime and to coordinate detection and prevention efforts against it. On a regional level, the organization *Europol* created the special *European Cybercrime Centre* (EC3) in The Hague in 2013, and quite recently made cybercrime a priority issue on its agenda.

The Center is hosted by Europol but was established by the European Commission to make the online world more secure for EU citizens. It is multifunctional: in addition to gathering and providing information related to cybercrime, it also supports cybercrime investigations and publishes threat assessments to raise awareness on general cybercrime issues, child sexual exploitation, and in particular payment card fraud. The center also cooperates with a wide range of other actors in detecting, responding to, and preventing cybercrime.

Did you know that ...

the European Cybercrime Centre has already supported more than seventy high-profile cybercrime operations?

Start of activities:	January 2013 (established by the European Commission)
Mandate:	Strengthen law enforcement response to cybercrime in the EU and help protect European citizens, businesses, and governments; tackle areas of cybercrime committed by organized groups to generate large criminal profits such as online fraud, other areas of cybercrime that cause serious harm to the victim such as online child sexual exploitation, and those areas of cybercrime including cyber-attacks that affect critical infrastructure and information systems in the European Union
Website:	https://www.europol.europa.eu/ec3
Twitter:	@EC3Europol

3. International Law and the Protection of Data and Privacy

Much of today's communication and commercial activities take place online. Still, most internet users are not aware of the many traces they leave behind when they buy something online, open a new email account, or create a profile on yet another social network site. They give away personal information – names, birth dates, addresses, phone numbers, and much more – on a regular basis. Furthermore, as the amount of data available online grows daily, so do the risks of the data being misused. Companies for instance trace their customer's activities online to provide them with tailor-made advertisement on other websites. But customers are not in all cases asked beforehand if they agree to share their information or for it be used for certain purposes, such as personalized advertising. Present-day technologies already allow for collecting, storing, and processing huge amounts of such data, which provide endless opportunities for different actors to exploit data sets for personal benefit. The problem is not only that actors are not transparent about what kind of data and how much data they really store, but also what they do with it. All these factors have a huge impact on the privacy of the customers.

One further consequence of the digital revolution is that people communicate more with each other than before: online, via email, personal messages on social networks, and communication apps on smartphones. The result is that a lot of power is currently concentrated in the communications sector. All of this digital communication has a global dimension, while much of it passes through the United States, where it is known that the government's *National Security Agency* (NSA) is overseeing and monitoring many activities of the population.

This mass surveillance is carried out through wiretapping and other spyware techniques. In 2013, the whistleblower *Edward Snowden*, a US computer specialist now living in exile in Russia, leaked numerous secret documents proving intelligence agencies' practices of intercepting communications and collecting communications metadata of US citizens and foreign nationals on a massive scale without informing them. The documents were published by well-known magazines around the world and accused the NSA of spying not only on citizens but also on other governments. Moreover, according to some documents, the NSA also deliberately attempted to weaken computer security, such as programs to encrypt data, thus putting the civil rights of millions of citizens as well as companies and other governments at stake. It is needless to add that other governments conduct related practices. The United Kingdom's Government Communications Head Quarters (GCHQ), for instance, is accused of tapping communications and storing metadata of millions of European citizens.

Which international and regional instruments protect data and privacy?

That the UK government was not transparent about authorizing its agency to store data led several British organizations to file a case before the European Court of Human Rights. They claim that this practice breaches their right to privacy under the European Convention on Human Rights, which holds that everyone has the right to respect for their private life and correspondence without interference by any public authority. In recent years, several rulings by international courts have held that the right to privacy extends to the online world and includes the protection of online data. In fact, a resolution of the United Nations General Assembly passed in July 2012 confirms that individuals have the same human rights online as offline.

chapter 9

Beyond the European Convention on Human Rights, a number of international human rights instruments provide for the protection of people's privacy and their data. Two of these are the Universal Declaration of Human Rights and the International Covenant on Civil and Political Rights (ICCPR).

On a regional level, the European Union is considered a front-runner in the field because it promotes a strong level of data protection, including personal data transfer outside the EU. In 1995, it adopted the *Data Protection Directive*, last amended in 2003, while it is planning to adopt the *General Data Protection Regulation* to unify data protection within its territory. The trend in EU policy is to provide citizens more control over their personal data, but at the same time to bring advantages for users and those who deal with the data. In contrast to the binding legislation adopted by the EU, the Association of Southeast Asian Nations (ASEAN) works with soft law instruments.

What challenges remain?

Even though numerous legal documents express the right to protection of private life, the debate on what privacy really means and includes is extensive and ongoing. It is about the willingness to share information about yourself and the decision on who has access to this information. It is about protecting your intimacy, your relational and spatial privacy. Therefore, it is also about the right to be left alone and the right to be free from the judgment of others. Despite all the risks that data storage and processing entails, it is clear that governments and intelligence agencies have an interest in gathering certain data to protect against threats posed, for example, by terrorism and cybercrime. But, as in so many circumstances, a balance needs to be found between protecting people's data and privacy and requiring surveillance and data collection for national security and law enforcement reasons.

Finally, privacy needs to be protected against more than government. The current debate on digitalizing health care, for example, highlights the risks of insurance companies or employers gaining access to this information and then basing their decisions for or against acceptance or employment on what they see in health records. The Internet thus enables not only governments but also commercial parties and other entities to exercise considerable (invisible) power over private citizens.

4. The Information Society: Copyright and Intellectual Property Versus Creative Commons and Open Source

Recent decades have witnessed a growth in the information available to society. The Internet is in fact full of information created or provided by people and organizations all over the world. Thus it is said that we live in an information society, in which strongly promoting and acting on freedom of information is seen as one of our fundamental human rights. The ICCPR, for instance, states that *everyone has the right to freedom of speech and expression*, which includes the freedom to seek, receive, and impart information through any media.

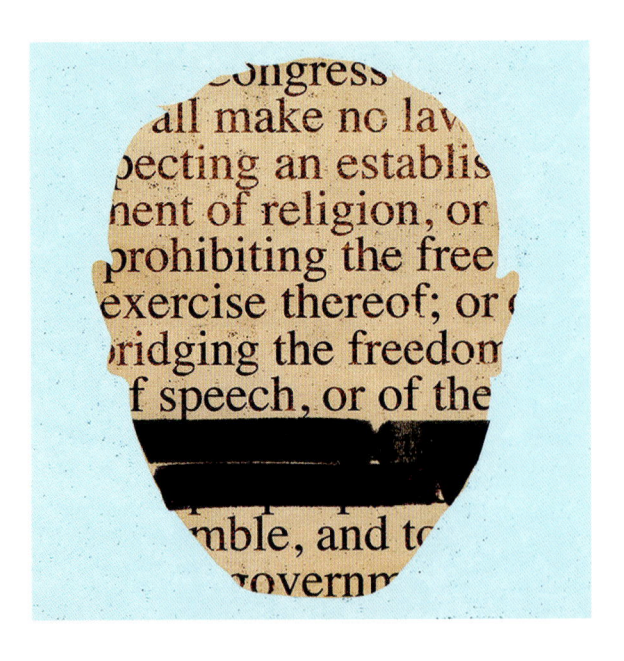

What challenges does the information society have to deal with?

The current challenge for international law is to develop standards that create a balance between complete openness and free use of information on the one hand and protection of the creators of such information on the other. Essentially every photo, text, video, or song being uploaded is protected by copyrights for those who created it. A blog post, for instance, is intellectual property of the individual who wrote and posted it and is therefore protected by copyright. Copyrights are rights given to authors or creators of certain work, under which they can give licenses to others allowing them to use or copy the work. This grants the authors and creators recognition and compensation for their work and encourages further innovation.

What does the law say on intellectual property?

In 1886, about a hundred years before the Internet was developed, the international community agreed on the *Bern Convention for the Protection of Literary and Artistic Works*, which was last amended in 1979. However, this document created only a minimum standard for the protection of copyright holder rights; the openness of the Internet meanwhile increased the probability of copyright infringements and exploitation of intellectual property. New instruments were therefore created on the regional and the international levels. In 1995, the World Trade Organization's *Agreement on Trade Related Aspects of Intellectual Property Rights* (TRIPS) came into effect. It is supposed to be the most comprehensive worldwide agreement on legal issues related to intellectual property. It entails a number of standards as well as enforcement procedures and dispute settlement mechanisms for disputes between World Trade Organization members on TRIPS-related aspects. A year later, the World Intellectual Property Organization adopted the *Copyright Treaty*, which now has ninety-three contracting parties. On a regional level, the EU adopted the *Directive on Copyright in the Information Society* in 2001, followed by the *Directive on Enforcement of Intellectual Property Rights* in 2004.

In contrast to agreements promoting the protection of intellectual property, others – in the context of promoting Internet freedom – highlight the right to freedom of information and with it the benefits of free access to and distribution of any kind of information. This idea is actually the core of the *open source* movement, which developed in recent years with mainstream use of the Internet. It means that the copyright holder of a product makes the instructions or programming code of the product available to the public, members of which then can change or further distribute the product as they see fit. The product might be software or perhaps a manual, for example. The benefits are that through distribution of information, cooperation increases and improvements of certain works or software is shared. The organization *Creative Commons (CC)* is based on the idea of open source, though with a focus on creative work. It aims at sharing creative work such as photographs, songs, or blog posts and it provides creators with CC licenses, in which creators define which rights they waive in order to give others the right to use and share the work.

Taking the right to freedom of information to its extreme, though, can also effectively put human rights at risk. The constant leaks of confidential government documents and classified information on the website *WikiLeaks* has been criticized not only by governments. It is one thing that the famous leak of diplomatic cables in 2010 endangers foreign relations between the U.S. and other governments, but WikiLeaks also published names of individuals involved in espionage, thus invading their personal privacy and putting their lives at risk.

5. On Liability for Freedom of Speech, Intermediaries, and E-Commerce

The Internet offers a great deal of room for wrongdoing, such as infringing copyrights or not respecting privacy rights. When these mistakes harm another person, the question is who is responsible (liable) and who is to pay the debts for the harm caused. This issue is relevant when false or confidential content has been published or distributed. The fundamental problem is that essentially anyone can create and spread any kind of content online, without first checking for correctness of content, and make it accessible to users everywhere. Some national legal systems hold a speaker liable for publishing wrong or insulting information, and this responsibility applies to online publication in the same way it does to conventional printed publication. This can include privacy violations, hate speech, or provocation to violence, to name just a few. One of the problems is that content that is lawful in one country may be unlawful in another.

Many states go as far as prohibiting any criticism against the government. This, however, challenges the *right to freedom of speech*. Various regional and international interpretations of that right therefore hold that governments may only limit this right and create liability if the limitation is clearly defined and necessary under a certain objective, such as national security or the endangering of public order. In addition, the limitation measures taken need to be proportionate to their goal.

The issue of liability becomes even more complicated when intermediaries are involved. Intermediaries are Internet service providers and webhosts, such as search engines or other platforms, host content that users produce. Such intermediaries are often called upon to help enforce copyrights, but they can also be subjects of lawsuits. According to current legal standards, these intermediaries can be held liable for spreading and hosting certain content and can be ordered to take the content offline. In May 2013, the *European Court of Justice* (ECJ) ruled on a case that concerned *"the right to be forgotten"* – another component of the right to privacy. At issue was *Google Spain's liability* for search results that violated the applicant's right to privacy. The applicant argued that the inaccurate and irrelevant information about him on the Internet should be deleted not only by the online newspaper, but also by Google, which should ensure that the information no longer appears in search results. The ECJ determined that owners of search engines can in fact be held liable because they exercise a certain control over personal data. The Court granted the applicant the right to ask Google to remove the links. The Court also stressed, however, that individuals have the right to such privacy only under certain conditions that must be assessed on a case-by-case basis.

Use of online intermediaries is also widespread in electronic commerce *(e-commerce)*. The Internet is an attractive forum for commercial activities because of its wide reach. Sellers can easily advertise and sell products and buyers have a mass supply from which to choose. The complication is that most online commercial transactions cross regional or national borders and when a legal dispute arises, it is not clear which law applies. In business-to-business commercial activities, the issue is less problematic because courts typically apply the *choice of law principle* for contracts and jurisdiction. When one party of a legal dispute on online commercial transaction is a consumer from another country, resolution is more complex. The lack of a single (uniform) approach can hinder access to justice for consumers or obstruct adequate protection of the companies' interests. In addition, in many cases the costs for litigation outweigh the costs of the products concerned.

How to overcome this lack of uniformity?

The EU is active in its effort to overcome this lack of a uniform legal approach. In 2012, it published the *Code of EU Online Rights* and, since 2014, the regular consumer protection laws also apply to online commercial activities. On the international level, though, rather than legally binding international standards, soft law instruments are in place, such as the guidelines adopted by the *Organisation for Economic Co-operation and Development* (OECD). Beyond these efforts, online communities to some extent also create their own rules and standards. Many websites today include a reputation system, in which users can leave comments and rate each other. Through these comments and ratings, considerable pressure can be brought to bear on users, encouraging them to do the right thing. The e-commerce company eBay is a good example. Noncommercial examples for these developments include Wikipedia, where it became a community standard that users may not publish or edit an article about themselves.

EQUAL JUSTICE UNDER LAW

International Criminal Law

Victims of the Cambodian and Balkan (civil) wars

International Criminal Law 7

What to expect from this chapter?

This chapter explores the development of international criminal law from its roots at the end of World War II through the era of ad hoc and mixed criminal tribunals to the establishment of the International Criminal Court (parts 2-4). The final section deals with recent cases and challenges to demonstrate the achievements of international criminal law (part 5).

1. Introduction

International criminal law is a special branch of public international law that applies to individuals rather than states. Under it, individuals can be convicted for committing an international crime. It is a relatively new specialty, developed only in the second half of the past century.

2. Development of International Criminal Law

Cooperation between states on criminal matters has been in place for quite some time. It includes, for example, co-operation in arrest warrants, extradition of suspects, transfer of sentences or proceedings, and recognition of judgments. The organization Interpol, which is active in supporting police forces around the world to fight transnational crimes, has existed since 1914. Its regional equivalent Europol began operations only in 1993.

The body of international criminal law today goes well beyond cooperation between states on criminal matters. It involves rules and procedures and international criminal institutions created to deal with alleged international crimes. These crimes include *war crimes, genocide, and crimes against humanity*, such as torture or sexual violence. International criminal law also regulates the *elements of these crimes* and different modes of liability. All this is based on the idea that there can be no crime or punishment without existing law (the principle of *nullum crimen sine lege*) and that people can be held responsible individually, whatever their function in a government, an army, or society at large.

The roots of international criminal law are deep in other international legal fields. War crimes, for example, have their origins in international humanitarian law, which encompasses the laws and rules of war and armed conflict. In fact, the substance of international criminal law is closely connected to humanitarian law, the core principles of which are proportionality, the distinction between combatants and noncombatants, the respect and protection for prisoners of war, and among other things the prohibition of torture. The rules of international

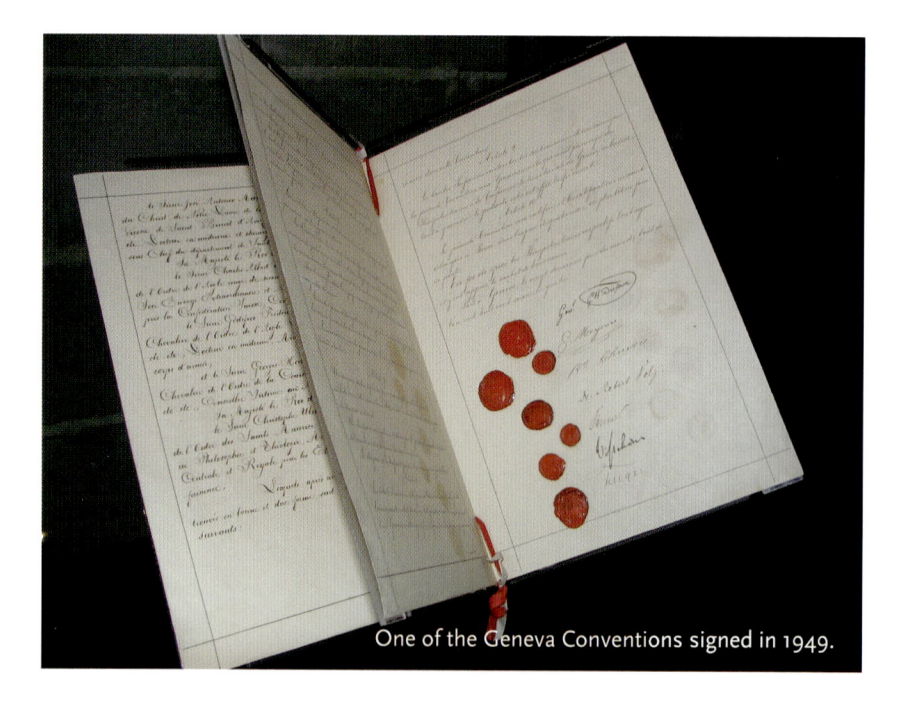

One of the Geneva Conventions signed in 1949.

humanitarian law can be found in international agreements, such as the Geneva Conventions of 1949 and the Protocols of 1977 thereto, or the Hague Regulations adopted at the *Hague Peace Conferences of 1907*.

The Trial at Nuremberg.

The first international criminal institutions were the Nuremberg and Tokyo Military Tribunals, set up in 1946 to deal with the atrocities committed during World War II and to prevent them from being repeated. The indicted individuals were prosecuted for crimes against peace, war crimes, and crimes against humanity. Before the tribunals were created, the only recognized international crimes were piracy and slave trading. These proceedings were thus a major step in the development of international criminal law. They have also been criticized, however, for being biased against the accused and as constituting victor's justice. All judges, as well as the prosecutor, were provided by the victor powers of World War II. Still, establishment of these two tribunals marked the first non-national prosecution and punishment of crimes with an international dimension and scope committed by high ranking military leaders and politicians.

3. Era of Ad Hoc and Mixed Criminal Tribunals

'Nuremberg' and 'Tokyo' laid the foundation for international criminal tribunals in the years to come. The next big step in international criminal law was in the 1990s, when the United Nations Security Council created two *ad hoc criminal tribunals*, that is, courts created for a special case or purpose. The first was the International Criminal Tribunal for the Former Yugoslavia (ICTY), which was given the mandate of trying those who had committed international crimes in the ethnic conflict between Bosnian Serbs and Bosnian Muslims and Croats in the territory of former Yugoslavia since 1991.

Prisoners in the yugoslav "concentration camps".

During that conflict, unimaginable crimes took place, such as mass murder, forced expulsion, systematic rape, and destruction of homes, land, and property. After photos revealing clear evidence of severe human rights violations which reminded of World War II were made public, the UN decided to send a group of experts to evaluate the situation. It determined that the Balkans presented a serious threat to international peace and security. The UN Security Council then adopted a resolution to set up the ICTY in The Hague.

Did you know that ...

the International Criminal Tribunal for the former Yugoslavia judges may call their own witnesses to the stand?

Established:	1993 by UN Security Council Resolution 827
Mandate:	Bring to justice those responsible for serious violations of international humanitarian law committed during the conflict in the former Yugoslavia and through this contribute to the restoration and maintenance of peace and security in the region
Jurisdiction:	Territory of the former Yugoslavia from 1991 onward, of individual persons only, concurrent with national courts
Number of judges:	10 (June 2016) including judges appointed for specific cases
Structure:	3 Trial Chambers, Appeals Chamber, Registry, Office of the Prosecutor
Staff:	550
First trial:	Tadic case (trial judgment in 1997)
As of June 2016:	161 accused
	19 acquittals
	83 convictions
Website:	http://www.icty.org/

In total, ICTY staff includes sixty-nine nationalities.

International Criminal Tribunal for the Former Yugoslavia (ICTY).

A year after the ICTY was launched the UN Security Council adopted another resolution establishing the *International Criminal Tribunal for Rwanda* (ICTR). Set up in the aftermath of the genocide in Rwanda, the tribunal's mandate was to prosecute those responsible. From April through mid-July 1994, barely one hundred days, more than eight hundred thousand Tutsi and moderate Hutu had been murdered by members of the Hutu majority. The creation of the ICTR followed for most parts that of the ICTY. The Rwandan tribunal is located in Arusha, Tanzania, and shares only an Appeals Chamber with the ICTY in The Hague. In addition, both tribunals also share the services of The Hague-based *UN Mechanism for International Criminal Tribunals* (MICT), which was established in 2010 to support the completion of their mandates. More specifically, the MICT supports and assists in managing the jurisdiction, rights and obligations, and other essential functions for both tribunals. It has supported the ICTR since July 2012 and the ICTY since July 2013.

Graveyard of the victims of the Rwandan genocide.

What other international criminal institutions are located in The Hague?

In 2006, for security reasons, the Charles Taylor trial under way in the *Special Court for Sierra Leone* was transferred from Freetown to The Hague. As the Sierra Leone civil war unfolded, Charles Taylor was president of Liberia. In 2003, he was accused of war crimes and crimes against humanity for his involvement in the Sierra Leone conflict. In 2012, Taylor became the first head of state convicted by an international court, specifically, for eleven counts of war crimes, crimes against humanity, and serious violations of international humanitarian law. After the closure of the Special Court for Sierra Leone in 2013, the Residual Special Court for Sierra Leone was established to continue the legal obligations of the former Court, such as witness protection, supervision of prison sentences, and management of archives of the Special Court.

Charles Taylor

Child soldier in Sierra Leone.

Since 2009, The Hague also hosts the *Special Tribunal for Lebanon* (STL), established under a joint agreement between the UN and the government of Lebanon. The tribunal deals with crimes that occurred in the attacks of 15 February 2005, which killed twenty-three people, including the former prime minister of Lebanon, and injured many others. It was also agreed that the tribunal has jurisdiction over crimes carried out at a later stage if they are related to those of February 2005.

Special Tribunal for Lebanon (STL).

The tribunal stands out for various reasons, one of which is that it is considered the first international tribunal to have jurisdiction over the *crime of terrorism*. This is especially interesting because at the moment no universally agreed definition of the crime of terrorism exists on the international level. The STL's statute includes only a reference to Lebanese law in that regard. The STL is also the first international tribunal to try crimes under national criminal law. In other cases – Cambodia, Iraq, and East-Timor, for instance – the combination of national and international law, as well as sometimes of national and international judges, prosecutors, and defense lawyers, has led to the terms *mixed*, *hybrid*, and *semi-internationalized* to describe these tribunals.

Did you know that ...

the Special Tribunal for Lebanon funding is 51 percent from voluntary contributions and 49 percent from the Lebanese government?

Established:	2007, operational in March 2009
Mandate:	Try persons responsible for the 14 February 2005 Beirut attack, other attacks in Lebanon between 1 October 2004 and 12 December 2005 if they are similar in nature and gravity and connected with the attack of 14 February 2005, and attacks carried out on any later date decided by the UN and the Republic of Lebanon, and with the consent of the UN Security Council
Number of judges:	11
Staff:	447
Structure/Chambers:	3 Chambers (pre-trial, trial, and appeals), a Registry, Office of the Prosecutor, Defense Office
Website:	http://www.stl-tsl.org/

There are many advantages to prosecuting crimes of such magnitude on the international level. That prosecutors, lawyers, and judges from all over the world are involved can make proceedings richer in expertise. A mix of nationalities also helps keep proceedings impartial, given that political manipulation is less likely, which is highly valuable given the scope and complexity of most international crimes. International criminal proceedings have also been criticized, however, for being too lengthy and costly, and for the fact that the actual proceedings often take place far from the crime scene and the victims. These circumstances might stand in the way of the restoration of peace and justice. This is also why mixed tribunals are situated either within the country where the crimes took place or at least close to the site of the crimes: the proceedings are more visible for the local community and victims are able to actually see the perpetrators being brought to justice.

Special Tribunal for Lebanon.

The opening of the new building of the International Criminal Court in The Hague.

4. The International Criminal Court

The criticism of international criminal proceedings being detached from the place of the crime is also raised against the *International Criminal Court* (ICC) in The Hague. The difference, however, is that the ICC – unlike special courts and tribunals – is a permanent international court. It was created to end impunity related to the more serious crimes of concern to the international community.

In July 2002, sixty states had ratified the Rome Statute, the Court's founding treaty, or *statute*. The biggest challenge during the drafting process was to find a balance between creating a strong and effective international organ and respecting the right and power of states to prosecute crimes themselves if they wish to do so. In the end, the participating parties agreed that the Court has jurisdiction over the crimes of *genocide, crimes against humanity, war crimes*, and potentially also the *crime of aggression*, if the state parties do decide to activate the Court's jurisdiction over such crimes in the future. The latter happened at the 2010 ICC Review Conference in Kampala. The Court's power to decide over such cases is in any case complementary, that is, the Court has jurisdiction only if states are not willing or able to take action themselves. This principle of complementarity is important to promoting criminal justice worldwide because it gives states an incentive to deal with cases in a manner acceptable to the international community and thus prevent the ICC from reviewing the case itself.

> On 19 April 2016 King Willem Alexander of The Netherlands opened the new ICC building, one of the most secured buildings in the world.

Did you know that ...

the International Criminal Court was initiated by Trinidad and Tobago's wish for international prosecution of drug offenses. Today the Court has no jurisdiction whatsoever over drug offenses?

Established:	1998, by the adoption of the Rome Statute, entered into force July 2002 after ratification by sixty countries
Mandate:	End impunity for individuals who committed serious crimes of concern to the international community as a whole, and contribute to the overall prevention of such crimes
Jurisdiction:	Crimes committed by nationals of a state party to the Rome Statute, or on the territory of a state party, or a state otherwise accepting the jurisdiction of the Court; situations referred by UN Security Council
State parties:	124
Number of Judges:	18
Number of staff:	800
Structure/Chambers:	Pre-Trial, Trial, and Appeals Chambers, President and 2 Vice-Presidents; Office of the Prosecutor, Registry
First case:	Thomas Lubanga Dyilo, Democratic Republic of the Congo
As of June 2016:	23 cases and 10 situations under investigation 8 preliminary examinations 29 arrest warrants 3 convictions 1 acquittal
Website:	www.icc-cpi.int

How do cases end up before the ICC?

First of all, state *parties to the ICC Statute themselves* can refer cases to the ICC. This has been done by Mali and the Democratic Republic of the Congo, for example. In April 2014, Ukraine, although not being a party to the ICC Statute, declared that it would accept the Court's jurisdiction for alleged crimes committed on its territory from 21 November 2013 to 22 February 2014. After such a referral or state declaration, the prosecutor opens a preliminary examination. Another possibility of bringing cases before the Court is that the *UN Security Council* acts under Chapter VII of the UN Charter, which happened with regard to Sudan and Libya.

Another option is in the *ICC prosecutor's power to initiate investigations*. In such an eventuality, the pre-trial chamber must decide whether enough evidence is available to start a case. This option has been criticized by many states, because it gives the prosecutor too much power, despite the need of support by the pre-trial chamber. At the moment, one-third of the UN member states remain outside the ICC, among them countries that claim large segments of the world's population, such as China, India, Indonesia, and the United States. Despite its failure to join, however, in practice the United States supports the ICC in many ways. For instance, it backed up the referral of cases by the UN Security Council by abstaining from voting in the case of Sudan (China doing the same) and voting in favor together with all other veto-powers and members in the case of Libya.

The relationship between the African Union (AU), which comprises fifty-four African states, and the ICC is somewhat troublesome. Some countries within the AU object to the ICC's ability to initiate proceedings, which led to the indictment of now serving head of state of Kenya, Uhuru Muigai Kenyatta, for alleged crimes against humanity during the country's 2007 national elections. In December 2014, the case was dropped basically because the Kenyan government failed to cooperate. The AU also accuses

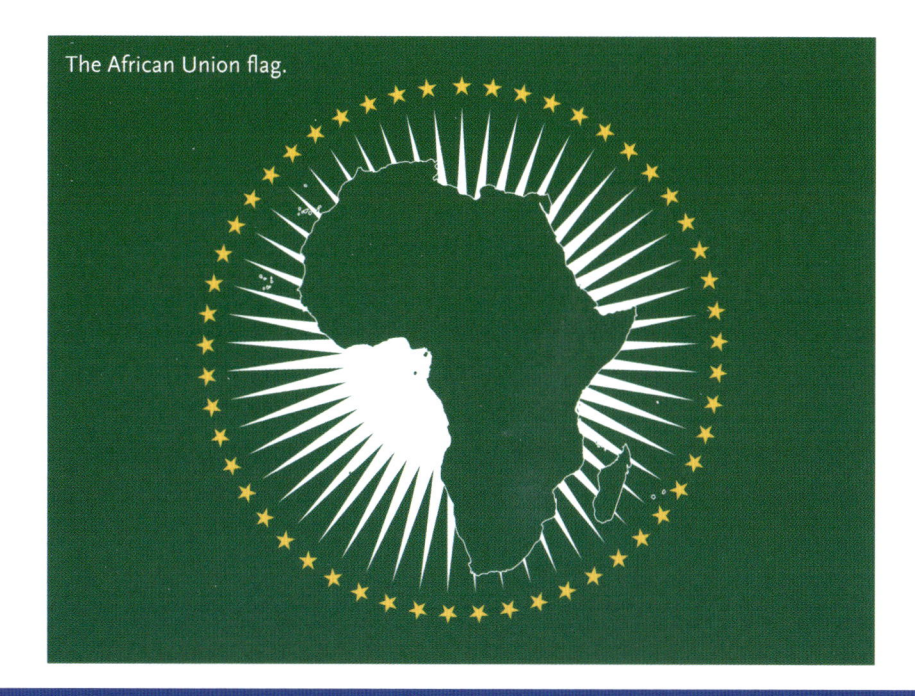

The African Union flag.

the ICC of being selective with its cases, in that all current situations under investigation and cases are in Africa. The AU argues that the ICC is selective in lifting immunities of sitting heads of states. One example is the arrest warrant issued against Sudanese President Al-Bashir for alleged crimes of genocide, crimes against humanity, and war crimes committed in Darfur, in the western part of Sudan.

Any resentment by a state has an influence on the willingness of states generally to cooperate with the Court. The ICC depends on this cooperation for the enforcement of its decisions and judgments, given that it has no enforcement mechanisms of its own. It also relies on states to execute arrest warrants and gather evidence and find victims. This dependency will remain one of the biggest challenges for the ICC in the years to come. In an interview with the authors of the present book in June 2014, ICTY President Theodor Meron commented on international criminal law in general:

> *"National judicial systems must be encouraged to develop the expertise and capacity to handle such cases […] much future work can and should be done at a national level."*

Here again, one can see the relevance of the above mentioned complementarity principle.

Darfur in the Western part of Sudan.

5. Achievements and Challenges of International Criminal Law

ICC president Judge Sang-Hyun Song once remarked that

"in an ideal world, our courtroom would be empty."

An empty courtroom, however, is not yet an option, because many states are not taking their own responsibilities seriously. Apart from that, the rules and norms of international criminal law are continuously being created and re-created by a network of international and semi-international courts and tribunals. This network has already succeeded in its trials of grave international crimes and several high-level individuals responsible for them, which has had a clear and positive effect on the development of international criminal law and in practice. For example, after the ICC's judgment against Thomas Lubanga Dyilo in 2012, in which he was found guilty of child soldiering, several guerrilla groups from the region released large numbers of child soldiers from their ranks.

What are the current challenges to international criminal law?

Despite achievements in international criminal law, the fact that quite some countries still do not accept the ICC's jurisdiction makes it clear how much work is yet to be done in promoting international criminal justice. One challenge, for instance, relates to the crime of sexual violence. It has come to be recognized more and more by different international tribunals and courts, even though prosecuting sexual violence is not always clear cut. In particular, because of the extended jurisprudence of the ICTY and ICTR, rape and other acts of sexual violence can now raise individual criminal responsibility under international law. And the ICC now also prosecutes rape, sexual slavery, enforced prostitution, forced pregnancy, enforced sterilization, gender based persecution, trafficking and other forms of sexual violence as crimes against humanity, war crimes, and genocide.

Another challenge is the inclusion of victims. In recent years, it has become more and more clear that victims can play instrumental roles in international criminal proceedings, but tend to be at risk when they do so. As ICTY President Theodor Meron further said at the interview:

> "Threats of retaliation and witness intimidation are still, sadly, all too common."

Involving victims in criminal proceedings is always a difficult undertaking, in part with regard to practical issues as translation, accommodation, and alike, but also with regard to their protection. Certain confidentiality and anonymity measures often need to be taken before testimony is given, which by definition entail procedural complications. Victim and witness protection is one of several essential functions entrusted to the MICT. Another is the victim's right to reparations, which is not recognized in all international criminal proceedings. At the Sierra Leone Tribunal, for example, victims are allowed to participate in the trials but cannot claim reparations. The ICC recognizes the victims' right to participate as witnesses and has set up a trust fund designed to provide individual victims and groups of victims with quick and easily accessible assistance.

Other challenges for international criminal justice include awareness raising and dissemination of knowledge. In many places where international crimes are committed, victims are not aware that international criminal proceedings can help them receive justice for the harm done to them. At the same time, in some cases victims' expectations may seem unrealistically high. The challenge for international criminal law then is to find a way to meet these expectations and bring about the desired justice. However, overly high expectations are without question problematic and perhaps the most significant challenge.

In general, international criminal proceedings receive more media attention and public awareness than other international legal issues. A prominent example is the case of Joseph Kony, the leader of the guerrilla group Lord's Resistance Army (LRA) in Uganda, which since 1987 has allegedly tried to violently overthrow the Ugandan government. In 2005, the ICC issued an arrest warrant for Kony, mentioning several counts of war crimes and crimes against humanity, including murder, enslavement, and forced enlistment of child soldiers. The warrant has still not been executed. In 2012, an American NGO launched a massive campaign for Kony's arrest; the campaign includes a video ranking among the most popular ones on YouTube. And even though it was the Ugandan government that referred the case to the ICC, the Court's involvement has been strongly criticized. First, the ICC has been blamed for not considering the atrocities committed by the Ugandan army in the fight against the LRA. Second, the launch of the ICC investigations is said to have interfered with the peace talks finally under way. In other cases as well, the ICC has been criticized for its efforts to seek justice in a society where peace does not exist. While balancing peace and justice, critics insist, the Court should bear in mind whose peace and justice are at stake.

The development of international criminal law is a recent one, after all. The launch of the ICC in 2002 has been described as one of the most innovative developments in international law since World War II. In the words of President Song,

> "Who would have thought twenty-five years ago that the prosecution of such crimes by an independent international institution would be the expected norm and not the exception?"

That might be a good way to express the core of the present chapter.

International Climate Law

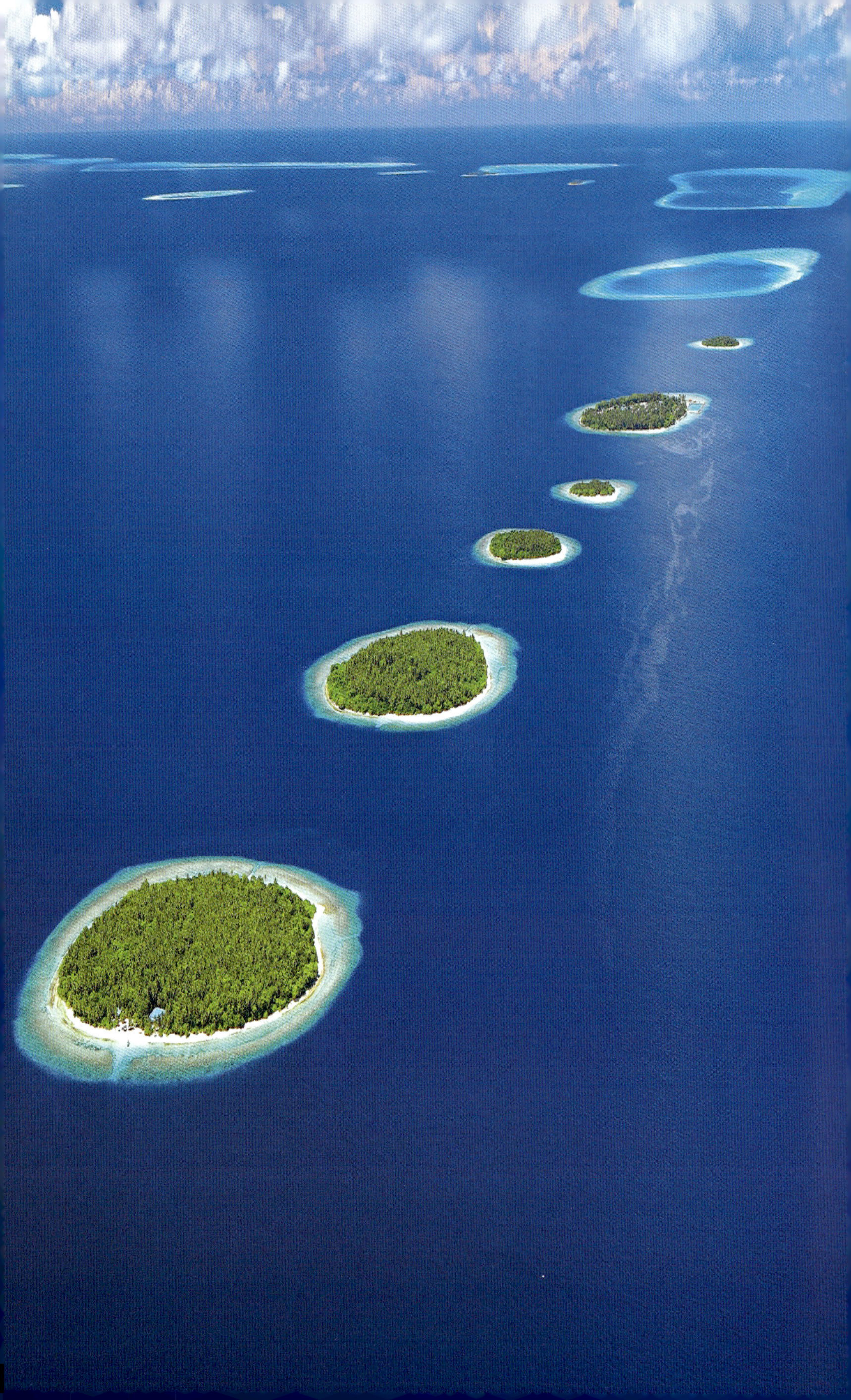

International Climate Law 8

What to expect from this chapter?

This chapter first briefly explains what climate change is and why international law is concerned with it. Part 3 discusses the actual laws on climate change, introducing international legal instruments and principles. Part 4 addresses the question of who is in fact responsible from a legal perspective for handling the multiple challenges related to climate change. Part 5 presents current examples of climate change lawsuits.

1. Introduction

Current generations, both young and old, are far more aware of environmental pollution than earlier generations, simply because people today have grown up knowing the trouble the environment is in and what it means to contribute to protecting it. This concern only found its way onto the agenda of the international community during the 1970s and 1980s. At that time, the alarm focused on the levels of pollution of rivers, oceans, and the atmosphere, the use of pesticides, and that an increasing number of animal species faced extinction. These concerns gradually led to the emergence of international environmental law, which – in a nutshell – regulates all human activity that might present a risk to the (that is, our) global environment. It operates through a network of treaties, regulations, declarations, and other instruments that all deal with specific areas of the environment, such as the oceans, the atmosphere, the climate system, or biological diversity. The biggest recent concern in environmental law is *climate change*.

2. About Climate Change Impacts and International Law

The past three decades are believed to be the warmest of the last thousand and a half years. In some regions, such as northern Alaska, temperatures have risen 3 degrees Celsius. On average worldwide, the combined air and water temperature is up almost 0.85 degrees Celsius. The energy added to the earth's energy system from this extra heat is equivalent to four hundred thousand Hiroshima atomic bombs exploding per day, every day of the year. The direct consequences and most obvious indicators of global warming are well known: melting glaciers, loss of ice mass in the Antarctic and Greenland, sea level rise, and increased and intensifying heatwaves and rainfall.

The overall impacts of climate change are much more diverse and far-reaching than a change in wind patterns and rainfall, however. Since 1988, the *Intergovernmental Panel on Climate Change* (IPCC) has been researching the various consequences and advancement of climate change. In its first report, the panel stated that climate change presents a growing risk to our environment, with consequences for everyone, everywhere on this planet. The report demonstrated that climate-related risks have an impact on human lives, ecosystems, societies, cultures, agriculture, other economies and industries, infrastructure, and much more. Certain regions already face water shortages, famines, and overall unsustainable livelihoods because of climate change. Estimates are that in 2013 more than twenty million people had been displaced by natural disasters. Like humans, certain animal species, both on land and in water, are also being forced to change their geographic range and seasonal habits.

Most of these impacts will only worsen as time goes by. The challenges will not only remain but in fact become greater and eventually lead to new challenges. One issue that makes this development clear is food security. When droughts and floods keep destroying land used for agricultural purposes (among other things), the decreases in crop yields can cause far-reaching famines. Consequently, even more lands will need to be transformed into agricultural fields if we are to have enough food to feed the growing world population. This also means, though, that more water will be needed for watering these fields, which aggravates existing water shortages. Furthermore, because of the supply shortages, prices for food and drinking products are likely to go up. The challenges connected to and triggered by the issue of food security are thus numerous. Why does international law deal with climate change?

This listing, which mentions only a few of the impacts of climate change, makes it clear that climate change is now – and will be even more so in the future – a source of numerous societal challenges. In contrast to most other environmental problems climate change truly is a global one and that is where international law comes in. Since the Industrial Revolution of the eighteenth and nineteenth centuries, not only the burning of coal, oil, and natural gas but also the marked growth in agricultural activity increased the emission of greenhouse gases (GHG), such as carbon dioxide, into the atmosphere. The problem today is that because of these gases, a growing proportion of the heat coming from the sun and radiated by the earth can no longer slip away into space, but instead is trapped in earth's atmosphere, leading to extra heat within the climate system. Put differently, more heat is coming in and staying in than is going out, which results in a continuous warming of the earth. The constant rise in releases of GHG into the atmosphere has the effect of adding yet another blanket. It does not matter where GHG are emitted because all emissions contribute to earth's overall climate. Research has proven, however, that if carbon dioxide emissions are reduced to a certain level, the impacts of climate change might not be as destructive as they seem to be at the moment. The 2015 Paris meeting on climate change suggests that an increase well below 2 degree Celsius is more or less acceptable and countries must work together to cut back on their emissions and achieve this temperature goal, while ideally limiting it to a 1.5 degree Celsius increase 'only'. This global nature of the impacts of climate change and the global approach required to deal with these impacts are what make international law the prime instrument for addressing climate change and achieving the necessary international cooperation.

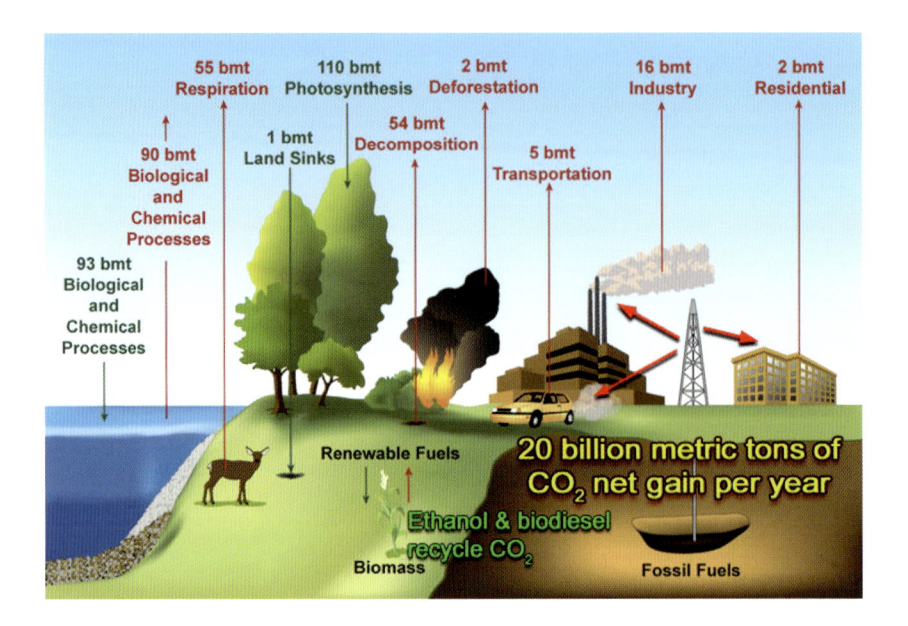

3. The Law on Climate Change

The increased awareness of the risks that global warming poses led to several bilateral, regional, and international legal instruments being adopted. One of the most important of these, adopted in 1992, is the *United Nations Framework Convention on Climate Change* (UNFCCC). With 195 parties states, the convention has near-universal membership. The convention recognizes the problem of climate change and lays out the key principles and methods of climate law. Its primary goal is a stabilization of GHG concentration in the atmosphere in order to prevent dangerous human interference with the climate system. According to the convention, this goal should be achieved within a certain time and without standing in the way of natural adaptation to climate change, and also without negatively affecting economic development and food production. The length of this period, however, is not specified in the treaty.

The UNFCCC builds on two pillars in addressing climate change: *mitigation* and *adaptation*. Mitigation means to ease or soften the effects of something. In the climate law context, mitigation refers to the efforts taken to reduce GHG emissions and minimize the harm done (such as emissions trading). Adaptation means to adjust or assimilate to certain conditions. Hence, adaptation measures in the climate context are designed for adjusting to climate-change impacts and learning how to live with the consequences. Since the Cancun *Conference of the Parties* (COP) in 2010 – the official decision-making body of the UNFCCC and made up of all state parties to the convention – the state parties have recognized that mitigation and adaptation are complementary activities, even though they operate differently with regard to time. Still, both have their advantages and disadvantages. Whereas adaptation measures do not really help weaken the impacts of climate change, mitigation measures are sometimes problematic because they can be difficult to combine with other issues, such as food security and agriculture. This consideration is also why adaptation measures have recently begun to play a more important role. Compared with mitigation, adaptation measures take on a more proactive approach to protecting ecosystems sustainably.

In 1997, the *Kyoto Protocol* (KP) was adopted, but because of a long ratification process it began operating only in 2005. The Protocol goes one step further – a major one – than the UNFCCC by committing developed signatory states to legally binding emission reduction targets. This commitment is also why it is often argued that the KP can be seen as the instrument through which the UNFCCC is being put into practice. In 1992, only thirty-seven states were considered developed countries. At the time countries with emerging economies – such as Brazil, Russia, India, China, and South Africa (BRICS) – did not yet have any legally binding reduction commitments. The reason it took so long to come into force is that the United States first participated actively and planned to join the agreement but reversed course with the election of a new president. This (negative) shift came after the sixth COP, which took place in November 2000 in The Hague.

Under the Protocol, the thirty-seven developed states committed to decrease their emissions between 2008 and 2012 (what was called the budget period) by 5 percent over 1990. A compliance committee, using regular reports and verification of emission levels, checked on countries to find out whether they lived up to their commitments. If a state

About The Hague Climate Conference (COP6, 2000)

... and why the US dropped out

At the sixth session of the COP, participants mainly discussed the implementation of the UNFCCC and the preparations for the implementation of the Kyoto Protocol. But the negotiations were affected by sensitive political issues, such as various disagreements between the United States and other countries. At some point, the European Union shared its resentment about the special treatment the US was receiving with regard to its emission reduction targets. Shortly after, the US declared that it would not join the Protocol.

emitted more CO_2 than allowed, it faced sanctions. Because of the failed negotiations at the Copenhagen COP in 2009, no legally binding emission reduction targets for after 2012 were agreed upon. Thus, since 2013 and until 2020, states have no legal obligation to cut back on emissions. Some states have voluntary commitments in place but whether these are being satisfied is in question.

What other legal methods are available?

Under the Kyoto Protocol, states are allowed to work together. One country can invest in another to achieve joint emission reductions, for example. This offers considerable flexibility for both states and companies in dealing with the new emission regulation. Based on this option, the EU developed an emission trading system, which permits companies to buy and sell emission allowances under an EU-wide emissions cap. This system provides economic and financial incentives to companies to cut back on their emissions. As the EU-wide cap automatically decreases over the years, the total amount of allowances available also decreases, which reduces the overall emissions across the EU.

Another option is the *Clean Development Mechanism* (CDM), a mitigation measure through which developed countries under the Kyoto Protocol can install what are called CDM projects in developing countries that contribute to both emission reduction and sustainable development. This measure earns countries more emission permits, known as *certified emission reduction credits* (CER). Such projects can, for example, involve installing solar panels in schools or electrifying a village through sustainable energy. The earned CER credits can then be sold to other countries. This brings more incentives and flexibility into the process of reducing emissions and simultaneously helps achieve development goals. At the moment, the count of registered projects is above seven hundred. The legal foundation of this mechanism is in Article 12 of the Protocol.

Achievements of the Clean Development Mechanism
Building the largest carbon offset instrument in the world

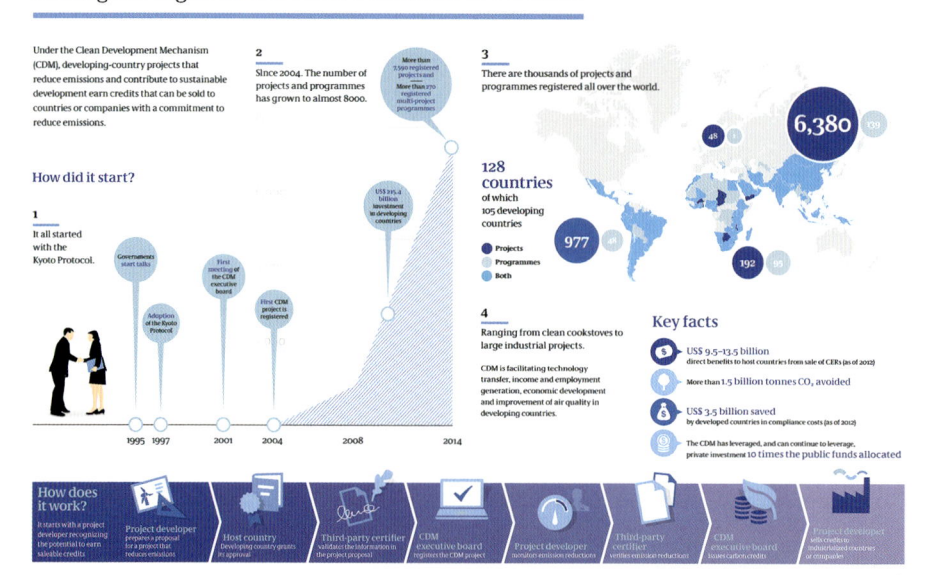

Scheveningen, The Netherlands, strengthening the dunes.

More detailed rules on developing, validating, and registering a CDM project were agreed on in the *2001 Marrakesh Accords.*

Numerous international, regional, and national policies on climate change adaptation are in place. The best known of these are efforts for raising and strengthening coastal defense to protect coastal zones from sea level rise and increased storm intensity. This also explains the infrastructural works at Scheveningen, the beach of The Hague, aimed at strengthening the dunes and the barrier dams at sea. That coastal zones are among the most vulnerable zones to climate change is common knowledge, and regional efforts such as those in the EU or the US acknowledge this threat to nature and lives of coastal communities. Another widespread adaptation measure is the creation of green spaces in cities to provide for more shade and reduce heat stress during heat waves. Evidence indicates that these green spaces have a cooling effect and thus help keep the temperature at an acceptable level. They also help in water management and preservation of biodiversity.

What legal principles are applicable?

Any method to address the issue of climate change is required to follow certain legal principles. Some are specifically designed for climate law; some also go back to general principles of international environmental law. One that does so is the precautionary principle, also referred to as the precautionary approach. It requires state parties to take immediate and positive action to mitigate and adapt to climate change, even if scientific evidence proving the positive or negative effect of such action is missing.

The principle of sustainable development also plays a role in environmental as well as climate law. It originates from the 1987 Brundtland Report and generally refers to the notion that one should strive for development that meets the requirements of the current generation but does not negatively affect the ability of future generations to meet their requirements. Applied to environmental law or climate law, it requires states to exploit resources sustainably and equitably – meaning that there must be enough for everyone, now and in the future.

Gro Harlem Brundtland

The principle of common but differentiated responsibility (CBDR) is also at the heart of the development of international climate law. While stipulating that all states have a duty to cooperate in curbing climate change, it acknowledges that industrial countries bear a larger responsibility in view of their historical record of greenhouse gas emissions and their financial and technological capabilities to mitigate these emissions.

Another concept of international environmental and climate law is the polluter pays principle, according to which actors who pollute or damage the environment are to be and must be held responsible for their actions. This principle is not included in the UNFCCC, but has been taken up by the Kyoto Protocol. In regard to climate change, it plays a particular role in lawsuits on climate change because it helps to answer the question of who is *liable* for the harm and what the appropriate remedy would be.

4. Developed vs. Developing Countries: Who Bears the Duty?

Legal efforts for dealing with the challenges of global warming have been affected by the North-South debate between developed and developing countries. In particular, the debate concerns the level of contribution to and responsibility for climate change. The Industrial Revolution helped developed countries achieve economic development but also led to an increase in greenhouse gas emissions, which is among the root causes of climate change. On the one hand are major developed countries, such as the US, reluctant to take legal responsibility and agree to reduction targets, despite being among the top emitters worldwide. In addition, China is considered a developing country under the UNFCCC and the Kyoto Protocol and therefore is not required to commit to emissions reductions. On the other hand are developing countries, such as some nations in Africa, Asia, or South America, which historically have contributed the least to climate change but now are expected to be the most affected by the impacts. More frequent droughts or more intense floods or storms negatively affect the world's poorest people and their efforts to improve their life conditions.

The dilemma is that, for quite some time now, developing countries have stressed their right to development and prioritized both improving their economic and social conditions and increasing their standard of living over climate change policies. Given the numerous challenges they face generally – such as poverty, poor health, and weak education systems – it becomes close to impossible for them to also deal with climate change. In

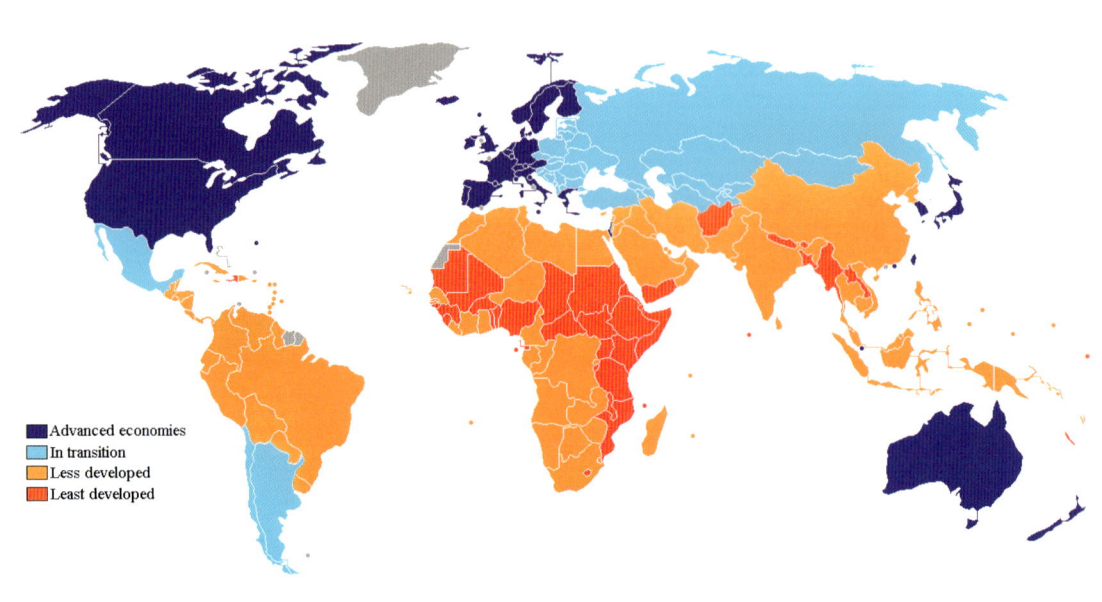

- Advanced economies
- In transition
- Less developed
- Least developed

fact, international law holds that all countries have a *common responsibility* to protect the environment, but given differing contributions to the problem in the past and differing abilities to take action against it and its consequences, this responsibility is *differentiated*, referring to the above mentioned principle on 'common but differentiated responsibilities'. In the climate law context, developed states are required to take primary responsibility for their historic contributions to the current situation, but at the same time developing countries must begin being responsible for their current and future contributions and not make the mistakes that developed countries made in the past.

The principle was first defined in the 1992 Rio Declaration on Environment and Development, but can also be found in the UNFCCC. It creates obligations for developed countries to lead the way in adopting mitigation policies and requires its parties to set up new funds for supporting developing countries with their climate change activities. The Kyoto Protocol can be seen as exemplary of the 'common but differentiated responsibilities'-principle in that it excludes developing countries from binding emission reduction targets. In fact, no binding obligations were imposed on developing countries for either the first commitment period, from 2008 to 2012, or the current period, from 2013 to 2020; only those developing countries who voluntarily committed have binding targets.

The problem is that developing countries are most affected by climate change and at the same time have the least ability and fewest resources to cope with it. This leaves some people more vulnerable to climate change impacts than others, which by definition associates climate change and climate law with human rights law, because a number of human rights are essentially endangered by climate change impacts. These are mostly those that depend to a certain extent on safeguarding natural resources: the right to life, the right to food, the right to health, and the right to development. In 2005, the Inter-American Commission on Human Rights dealt with a case that concerned the living environment of the *Inuit people in the Arctic*. Climate change impacts make it extremely difficult for the Inuit to access vital resources and to pursue their cultural traditions. The loss of ice limits their fishing and hunting and even leads to loss of their homes. The Inuit filed a petition accusing the Canadian government of violating their human rights by failing both to reduce greenhouse gas emissions and to adopt adequate measures against climate change. Although the commission determined that the application was inadmissible, the petition nevertheless helped raise awareness about climate change and the adverse impacts it can have on human rights, in particular for vulnerable groups.

chapter 9

The Inuit people.

5. Climate Change Liability

Recent years have seen a general increase in the number of lawsuits motivated by climate change issues. This is true for international legal institutions such as the International Court of Justice, the Permanent Court of Arbitration, the Inter-American Court of Human Rights, and the European Court of Human Rights, all of which deal with more and more cases which are directly or indirectly related to environmental or climate law. On the national level, the number of lawsuits in which individuals try to hold governments *liable* for their actions or inactions in relation to climate change has also increased. In 2011, the first civil cases on climate change were brought in the United States against state governments. The suits were brought by the nonprofit organization Our Children's Trust on behalf of minors, and claimed that the government has failed to protect the atmosphere from climate change impacts and therefore put their future lives at risk. The attorneys based these lawsuits on the principle of intergenerational equity, which basically holds that natural resources and the climate system need to be preserved not only for present but also for future generations. This principle is also incorporated in the UNFCCC, which requires state parties to protect the climate system *"for the benefit of present and future generations."* Until now, none of these cases have been successful, but the degree of legal action constantly rises and has motivated lawsuits in other countries, such as Uganda, the Philippines, and Ukraine.

The Urgenda judgment.

Another national lawsuit on climate change has been heard recently in the district court in The Hague. In 2013, the Dutch foundation Urgenda brought a suit against the state of The Netherlands, arguing that the Dutch government did not implement enough measures to reduce greenhouse gas emissions and was legally accountable for not taking enough action against a foreseeable harm against its citizens. According to Urgenda, this situation constitutes a *wrongful act of state*. In June 2015, the Court ruled that the Dutch state must take more action to reduce its greenhouse gas emissions and ensure that Dutch emissions will be at least 25 percent lower by 2020 than they were in 1990. It is the first European case in which citizens have tried to hold the government responsible for inaction related to climate change. The Dutch state instituted an appeal against the judgment. Looking at the overall trend, it is not likely to be the last one. The rise in climate change lawsuits led to an increased public awareness about the challenges surrounding the issue. If the number and variety of these challenges make one thing clear, it is that we all can contribute to improving the situation and to being able to live with a changed climate. Even though the evidence is clear, however, tensions remain between what is considered to be necessary action and how far different states are willing to go to increase international cooperation on climate change.

Climate change does not only affect human beings

Human Rights Law

French Declaration of the Rights of Man and of the Citizen, 1789.

Human Rights Law 9

What to expect from this chapter?

This chapter first presents the background of the notion of human rights and addresses developments until World War II and in part 3 it describes some of the main characteristics of international human rights law today. Part 4 addresses three issues in the efforts for the further universalization of human rights: the leeway that states have to "do it their own way," the existence of cultural relativism, and the limits to sovereignty. Two topical issues wrap up the discussion: part 5 explores the protection of vulnerable groups and part 6 addresses the interplay of companies and human rights.

1. Introduction

Every person on the planet is born equal and free in dignity and rights. These rights are human rights, which can be seen as a package with two basic components: protecting people against abuse of governmental power, and – parallel to that – requiring that those who hold political and economic power help in ensuring *human dignity* for all people worldwide. In standard human rights terminology, states and nonstate actors such as companies must realize *civil* rights such as to freedom of religion, *political* rights such as to vote, *economic* rights such as to social security, *social* rights such as to adequate housing, and *cultural* rights such as to enjoy cultural identity and to protect traditions.

ture page 173: Syrian refugee at the European border.

The Magna Carta of 1215, British Library.

2. A Short Historical Note

The history of human rights is often linked to the *Magna Carta* of 1215, the document with which England's King John responded to complaints about his abuse of power. This document is usually coined as the symbolic point of departure, but in fact the history of a variety of human rights can be traced even further back in time and relates not only to civil and political rights but also to economic, social, and cultural rights. However, the Magna Carta helped make clear that rulers were subject and accountable to the law rather than the citizens to the ruler. In 1581, this idea found its way to the magistrates of the Union of Utrecht in the Netherlands, who signed in that year a document in The Hague that denounced King Philip II of Spain for oppressing his subjects and denying them their rights. The real breakthrough of that idea, however, would come only several centuries later. During the Enlightenment, in the seventeenth and eighteenth centuries, people began to more systematically claim their rights as human beings rather than acknowledge any absolute power of governments and kings. Documents such as the French Declaration of the Rights of Man and of the Citizen (1789) and the US Bill of Rights (1791) were the result of these claims, for which thinkers such as John Locke (1632–1704), Jean-Jacques Rousseau (1712–1778), and Immanuel Kant (1724–1804) had provided the underlying arguments.

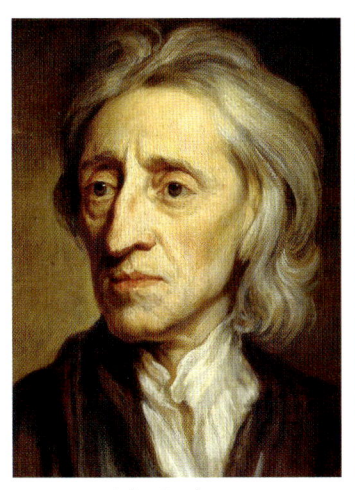

John Locke

Jean-Jacques Rousseau

Immanuel Kant

At that time, however, protection of human rights was not included in national documents. The first signs of international protection of human rights date from considerably later: the late nineteenth century and the beginning of the twentieth. At the Brussels conference of 1890, for example, an international antislavery agreement was adopted and at the *Hague Peace Conferences of 1899 and 1907* about fifteen agreements addressing the humanitarian aspects of wars and international dispute settlement were signed. Also at that time, the first agreements appeared for the protection of national minorities. These included the 1878 Treaty of Berlin, in which Balkan states such as Bulgaria, Montenegro, Serbia, and Romania were required to observe freedom of religion for the Muslim minorities in Bulgaria and Montenegro and the Jewish minority in Serbia and Romania. The 1919 *Covenant on the League of Nations*, predecessor of the *United Nations* (UN), included a number of articles relating to matters such as the human labor conditions and the protection of national minorities. In the same year the International Labour Organization was established as the first international social affairs institution.

The real breakthrough in the *international* protection of human rights and in including human rights in written international agreements (codification), is linked to the establishment of the UN, which was founded in response to the atrocities of World War II. In response the large-scale violations of human rights during the war, states placed protection of these rights high on the international agenda. A key moment in that history was US President Roosevelt's *Four Freedoms speech*, which he delivered in 1941. His focus on the combination of the freedom of religion, free speech, freedom from want (which might now be called 'providing for basic needs'), and freedom from fear inspired the drafters of the UN Charter. It is important to remember, however, that human rights were included in the Charter not only because states wished to include them, but also in response to the pressure of nongovernmental organizations.

President Roosevelt's Four Freedoms speech, 1941.

3. Towards modern Human Rights Law

In 1946, the United Nations established the UN Commission on Human Rights, later on replaced by the UN Human Rights Council (2006). The Commission, led by Eleanor Roosevelt and René Cassin, drafted the 1948 *Universal Declaration of Human Rights*, which is still the basis of all human rights documents. The Declaration first makes clear that human rights must be seen as universal ↗: they apply to all human beings, regardless of where they come from, where they live, or what they do. Next, the Declaration clarifies what human rights are all about, providing an overview of all civil, political, economic, social, and cultural rights.

Eleanor Roosevelt and the Universal Declaration of Human Rights, 1948.

The Declaration did not, however, establish legal obligations for states. This came about with the adoption of a series of international human rights treaties. Some of these are rather broad, such as those relating to civil and political rights (1966) and to economic, social, and cultural rights (1966). Others address specific themes: racial discrimination (1965), torture (1984), enforced disappearances (2006). Still others focus on specific groups: women (1979), children (1989), migrant workers (2003), and persons with disabilities (2007). Signatory states are bound by them because they consent to be bound. ல However, quite a number of human rights norms are also binding even if states do not express their wish to be bound. They are *binding upon states whether they like it or not*, either because these rights are customary international law ல, or because they are "peremptory standards" ல of international human rights law, also known as *ius cogens* ல standards. Two critical examples are the ban on genocide and torture, which are covered by the 1948 *Convention on Genocide* and the 1984 *Convention on Torture*, respectively.

UN human rights supervisory bodies ல see to it whether states live up to their human rights obligations. These bodies comment on reports made by states about the realization of human rights and react to complaints filed by individuals on certain human rights standards. In addition, they present what are called General Comments, in which they further specify the character of the human rights standards under their supervision. The UN human rights supervisory bodies regularly meet in Geneva. In addition, international organizations based in The Hague have played a major role in applying human rights standards as well. These include, among other ones, the International Criminal Tribunal for the former Yugoslavia, the International Court of Justice (ICJ) and the International Criminal Court (ICC). Although the ICJ does not have a specific human rights mandate, human rights law is part of the larger domain of international law. In the above mentioned 2004 Advisory Opinion on the legality of the Israeli wall, for instance, the ICJ made clear that the construction and operation of the wall leads to a number of human rights violations of Palestinians, both individually and as a people, such as free movement and self-determination. In another case, the ICJ ruled in 2007 that though Serbia did not actually commit the genocide in Bosnia-Herzegovina, it nevertheless violated its obligation to prevent it and to punish the perpetrators of the crimes.

chapter 2 and chapter 7

The Srebrenica Genocide Memorial in Potocari.

How can individuals claim human rights?

That human rights standards are more or less clear and that human rights law is in many ways internationalized does not mean that those suffering from the violations of such standards automatically have access to international and regional courts and committees. State governments are first of all responsible for including internationally set standards of human rights protection into national law, and it is basically still up to them to allow their citizens and other people under their legal power access to such international bodies. That can easily evolve into a vicious circle: governments responsible for human rights violations are often not willing to give victims of such violations access to regional or international supervisory bodies. The converse is true within the Council of Europe, which now comprises forty-seven European states. Within the Council, all victims of human rights violations have access to the *European Court of Human Rights* as long as they have used all national legal remedies (and met a few other criteria, not relevant to this context). Under UN human rights treaties, however, states are not obliged to grant their citizens and

The European Court of Human Rights in Strasbourg

other people under their legal power access to international complaint procedures. States can become a party to international human rights treaties but leave out the option of access to complaint procedures. All UN member states, however, are subject to the *Universal Periodical Review* (UPR) organized by the UN Human Rights Council. Separately, the UN is also *mainstreaming* human rights in other domains, such as peace and security and development. For that reason, it is sometimes said that human rights are *the* lodestar of the organization.

4. Limits to State Sovereignty

Within existing international human rights law, states have some *space to comply with human rights standards in their own way*, they have – as it is known in international law – a *margin of appreciation*. Ideally, use of that margin is supervised by independent third bodies such as human rights courts and committees or the Human Rights Council using its Universal Periodic Review mechanism. The margin of appreciation allows states to apply their political, economic, social, and cultural particularities and differences. Ignoring these would be unrealistic given that each state has its own history and particular difficulties. Some states are very young and have numerous concerns in addition to strictly human rights concerns. Other states are trying to put an end to a left-wing or right-wing dictatorial past and cannot do so from one day to the next.

The margin of appreciation becomes problematic, however, if states are clearly abusing their margins, do not want to be controlled by supervisory bodies, or question human rights standards as such. The latter is also called '*human rights relativism*', the mirror image of universality of human rights standards. On the one hand, respecting cultural differences can lead to a situation where the realization of human rights is strongly limited or even sidelined because of certain cultural traditions or values that play an important role in a particular culture. Examples are *female genital mutilation* and not allowing female heirs to have a share in the *legacy* after the decease of the father. In human rights terms, the first would qualify as inhumane treatment, and the second as discrimination against women.

Taking such cultural differences into account – as a starting point – while discussing the underlying arguments used by different actors in such cultures can and should help – in the end – in fitting human rights into all cultures. This phenomenon is also known as the *localization of human rights*, as part of a process-oriented strategy leading to the *universalization* of human rights and ensuring these rights in a tailored way in all cultures.

Can states still argue that they do it their own way?

Are states still in a position to claim that their way of dealing with human rights is a matter of *domestic concern* and thus of their *sovereignty*? That is, to what extent can they say to others, especially governments and nongovernmental organizations, that they should *mind their own business*? The development of law in recent decades makes it quite clear that states cannot do what they like in regard to human rights. Sovereignty is limited and *comes with responsibilities.* Although the UN Charter limits the protection of national sovereignty to matters that "essentially fall within the domestic jurisdiction of States," it is now clear that the protection of human rights is a *legitimate concern of the international community*, as the final document of the 1993 Vienna World Conference on Human Rights explicitly states. The phrase has been repeated since then in a range of UN documents and invoked in numerous cases. The universality and universalization of human rights nonetheless have a long way to go and need to be achieved time and time again in everyday turbulent political contexts.

5. Protecting Vulnerable Groups

Everywhere around the globe are people who belong to a particularly vulnerable group. *Children*, for example, are considered to be among the most vulnerable in our societies whether in peace or conflict. To illustrate: these days over one billion children live in countries affected by armed conflict.

Refugees or stateless people are also particularly vulnerable. Refugees are currently high on the agenda of the international community. Civil wars and natural catastrophes cause millions of people to flee their home countries. Many are now seeking refuge in Europe. On their dangerous journeys, these people are often living in hazardous conditions or exploited by traffickers who smuggle them into other countries for money. Together with other displaced persons, refugees fall under the mandate of the *International Organization for Migration* (IOM), which works to ensure orderly and humane management of migration. The Dutch branch of IOM is located in The Hague, as is the Dutch office of the *United Nations Refugee Agency UNHCR*. Since its establishment in 1950, the agency's task is to safeguard the rights of refugees and lead and coordinate international action for the protection of refugees. Today, it is based in 123 countries with more than 9000 staff members.

In many cases, vulnerable groups face discrimination and violations of their right to political recognition and participation. Each of these groups, and the individuals belonging to them, have been offered a room in the house called "international (human rights) law" but it is quite clear that the legal protection is either still not enough or at best still in process. *Indigenous peoples* are particularly vulnerable. Well-known examples include the Masaai in Kenya, the Aboriginals in Australia, and the Inuit in Canada. According to the UN, the worldwide count of indigenous communities worldwide is approximately five thousand. These peoples share a culture and history, want to be seen as indigenous, and have been attached to a particular territory for time immemorial. In 2007, after decades of discussion, the UN adopted the Declaration on the Rights of

Masaai in Kenya.

Indigenous Peoples, which is generally seen as a milestone, even if the implementation ⌇ of the Declaration is only in its infancy.

What rights do these groups have?

While adopting the 2007 declaration, the UN also confirmed the notion of collective or group rights. In contrast to individually oriented human rights, these rights belong to a group of people and sometimes to peoples as a whole as well as to individuals. Group rights are especially important for *national minorities*. Examples include the Catalans and Basque people in Spain, the Quebecois in Canada, and the Frisians in the Netherlands. No agreement has been reached on what defines a national minority, but generally the term describes a group of people distinct from the majority of population on the basis of religious, cultural, linguistic, or ethnic differences.

One particularly significant right of peoples is that to self-determination.⌇ It is a people's right in the sense that it is a collective or group right allowing peoples to decide their own destiny. It allows peoples to freely determine their political status and achieve economic, social, and cultural development according to their will. Under certain conditions, this can entail the right to establish an own state (*external self-*

Catalans demonstrating for their rights.

determination), but regularly it means autonomy within an existing state, such as having a different official language (*internal self-determination*). The right to self-determination is recognized in many international and regional legal instruments and arose from normative resolutions of the General Assembly of the UN such as the famous *Decolonization Declaration* of 1960. The International Court of Justice has dealt with a number of self-determination cases. One well-known example is that of Kosovo, which in 2008 declared independence from Serbia. Given an unclear legal situation, the UN General Assembly asked the ICJ for an *advisory opinion*. The Court found that Kosovo had not violated international law in proclaiming an independent state, but did not take any position on the question whether the move was legally justified. The Court's decision was relevant primarily to the conflict between Serbia and Kosovo, but has been looked at with great interest by independence movements worldwide.

The presence of minority groups is occasionally felt as a threat to internal peace and security. That might be so for a variety of reasons, whether because individuals within these groups are prevented from integrating and participating in the political, social, economic, or cultural life of a country, or because their leaders prefer to join the state that comes closest in terms of ethnicity (the *kin state*), or because these leaders want to separate regardless, with or without factually sound reasons. The result of these tensions can be unrest and even violent conflicts, which can bring about manifold human rights prices to be paid. To prevent this situation from arising, some international organizations focus on protecting rights of national minorities and strengthening mutual acceptance within a country. One is the *Organisation for Security and Co-operation in Europe (OSCE)*, which comprises fifty-seven states and takes a broad approach to security, including politico-military aspects, economic and environmental aspects, and human rights. After the fall of the Berlin Wall in 1989, its predecessor, the Conference on Security and Co-operation in Europe, installed a High Commissioner on National Minorities on the initiative of the Dutch government. The office of the High Commissioner is located in The Hague.

Astrid Thors, High Commissioner since 2013

About the OSCE High Commissioner on National Minorities

Established:	December 1992, office opened January 1993
Mandate:	Instrument of conflict prevention at the earliest possible stage; identify and help solve ethnic tensions that might endanger peace, stability or friendly relations among OSCE states
Website:	http://www.osce.org/hcnm

The High Commissioner's role is to provide early warning and take appropriate action to prevent ethnic tensions from developing into a conflict, by promoting mutual understanding, integration, and participation for minority groups, but also by providing education in minority languages. The key is silent diplomacy and building relations in confidence with governments, minority representatives and other actors. The High Commissioner does not conduct investigations into individual cases of human rights abuses. Instead, the Commissioner engages in on-site missions to assist governments by publishing recommendations, guidelines, and best-practice examples on how to resolve conflicts with national minorities and prevent them from becoming a security threat.

6. Companies and Human Rights

Other actors besides states – that is, nonstate actors – have come to play an important role in protecting and ensuring human rights. This is especially true of companies, which in the wake of globalization have sought ways to optimize their business operations to stay competitive. The results are that multinational enterprises, such as garment companies H&M and GAP, rely extensively on workers and supply from abroad, where labour is often cheaper and production costs lower, and where sometimes national law does not require the same respect for human rights as the company's home country does. The likelihood of human rights abuses by companies therefore rises constantly and *businesses need to be aware that their operations can and often do affect a series of human rights*, whether political, civil, social, economic, or cultural. Certain activities can even violate group rights, as when indigenous peoples are displaced to make room for a new production site.

A high-profile issue is the booming phenomenon of private military and security companies (PMSCs), some of which have been accused of unlawful use of force against civilians in conflict areas. One prominent example is the company best known as Blackwater, whose employees allegedly killed and wounded civilians in Iraq in 2007 without provocation; the company has changed its name several times since then. *Business-related and mega-sporting events*, such as the Olympic Games or the FIFA World Cup, have also become more and more a concern for human rights advocates. The workers hired to build the necessary infrastructure for hosting the event, which in many cases are migrants from nearby countries, are typically exposed to poor (or worse) working and living conditions. Displacement of groups of people to make way for sporting venues is also documented.

A tragic example of corporate violation of human rights is an incident in the spring of 2013, when the eight-story Rana Plaza building collapsed on 24 April in Savar, a city in the middle of Bangladesh. A variety of banks, stores, apartments, and garment factories producing goods for Benetton, Mango, Primark, Walmart, and the Children's Place, were located inside the building. Until a day before the collapse, complaints and concerns had been lodged about cracks in the walls and the instability of the building. Allegedly, the factory manager and other company officials said it was safe to enter the building, forcing employees – threatened with a one-month salary cut – to return. When the building collapsed in the morning hours, 1,129 people died and more than 2,500 were injured in one of the deadliest factory accidents in modern history. Only a year later did victims and families of injured or dead workers begin to receive compensation. Some companies are covering the payments from their own funds. Others rely on a trust fund set up by the International Labour Organization (ILO).

Rana Plaza building.

The *ILO* is one of those international organizations that over the years have become more and more active in addressing the challenge of business and human rights by continuously emphasizing the need to respect *core labour standards* – freedom of association, collective bargaining, elimination of all forms of forced labour, elimination of child labour, and elimination of discrimination. These norms are included in the *human rights conventions* of the ILO, to which all 185 member states must adhere. In 1998, the ILO also adopted its Declaration on Fundamental Principles and Rights at Work, which further supports the same principles (sometimes also called minimum or core labour norms).

Another international organization active in business and human rights is the *Organisation for Economic Co-operation and Development*, which now includes thirty-four industrialized nations. In 1976, it adopted *Guidelines for Multinational Enterprises*, last updated in 2011, which comprise recommendations to multinational enterprises on how to operate responsibly with respect to applicable rules and laws. The guidelines play a major role in defining the human rights responsibilities of companies.

The newest asset in this field are the *Guiding Principles on Business and Human Rights* adopted by the UN in 2011. This international legal framework for business and human rights is structured along *three pillars*: the duty of states to protect human rights, the corporate responsibility of companies to respect human rights, and the provision of effective remedies for victims of human rights abuses. The framework has been criticized for representing numerous compromises, but it has also led to further action. The UN Working Group that oversees the realization of the Principles took up efforts by the European Commission calling on states to present *National Action Plans* about what they do with regard to businesses and human rights and the UN Principles. In December 2013, the Dutch Ministry of Foreign Affairs presented the Dutch National Action Plan, one of the first countries to do so. The plan highlights the governments' priorities in implementing the guiding principles, focusing on amongst other things the active role of the government and its duty to protect, the importance of policy coherence, due diligence, transparency, and effective remedies.

Can individuals bring human rights lawsuits against companies?

Recently, a number of states launched a discussion on *drafting a treaty on business and human rights*. Whatever the outcome, it is clear that so far no international organization or mechanism exists that allows victims to sue a company. Until today, *national tort law* has been used in a range of cases to fill the gap because tort is an open criterion. The general problem, however, is that in most cases it is difficult to establish whether victims have access to a certain national court in relation to the respective act. Key questions are *where* the harmful act took place, *what nationality* the victims have, and *under which law* the company in question operates. What can complicate the situation even more is when a subsidiary company rather than the parent company has violated the rights of workers or people living in the company environment. This was the case in Nigeria in 2008. Five Nigerian farmers argued that poor maintenance of the Dutch oil company Shell and its Nigerian subsidiary led to an oil spill that caused them to lose their livelihood. With strong support from civil society through several nongovernmental organizations, especially Friends of the Earth, the farmers brought the case before the district court in The Hague, which in 2013 decided that the Nigerian subsidiary had to pay compensation to one of the farmers. The case is now on appeal. In December 2015, the Court of Appeal in The Hague decided that Dutch courts have the right to look at the case, which means that one can now also look at the claims of the remaining farmers. Awaiting the outcome, it has become clear that lawsuits in principle can be brought against companies when individual human rights are violated. This said, the case is also only one of a few. Business and human rights are yet another challenge for human rights law. It is the commitment of many states and numerous nongovernmental, national, regional, and local organizations to address those challenges with a common goal: to end human rights violations by whatever actor and ultimately ensure the enjoyment of human rights for all individuals and groups across the world.

Law of the Sea

Shipping routes

Law of the Sea 10

What to expect from this chapter?

First, some historical background is provided, including efforts to codify the international law of the sea (part 2). Next, the 1982 UN Convention on the Law of the Sea is reviewed (part 3). Furthermore, the mechanisms to settle maritime disputes are discussed and reference is made to some recent disputes (part 4).

1. Introduction

One of the most interesting and highly developed areas of public international law is the law of the sea. The seas and oceans form two thirds of the surface area of our planet. Nowadays, they are intensively used for all kinds of purposes including navigation, fisheries, overflight, trade and oil and gas exploitation. For centuries customary international law prevailed. In the period of the United Nations a comprehensive law of the sea convention was concluded, often referred to as the Constitution for the Oceans. It has substantially extended territorial sovereignty over neighboring maritime areas.

2. Historical background

Ideas on the use of the sea go back millennia. The Romans, for example, did not consider the sea to be suitable for division as private property, although they did refer to the entire Mediterranean Sea as their own sea – *mare nostrum*. In his renowned book, *Mare liberum* (1609) Hugo Grotius advocated freedom of the sea and dismissed Portuguese claims to the sea route to Asia and British claims to the sea surrounding Britain.

Various publications related to the "Mare Liberum".

In 1703, the Dutchman Cornelis van Bijnkershoeck published a celebrated work on the law of the sea entitled *De dominio maris dissertatio* (treatise on sovereignty of the sea). In this book he explained what he saw as the two cornerstones of the law of the sea: the freedom of the high seas and the territorial sovereignty of coastal states over an area of the sea that could be defended from the coast (the 'cannon shot rule'). However, it was not until the nineteenth century that the principle of freedom of the high seas received full and general recognition. This was understood to apply in particular to shipping, international trade and fishing.

Statue of Van Bijnkershoeck, The Hague.

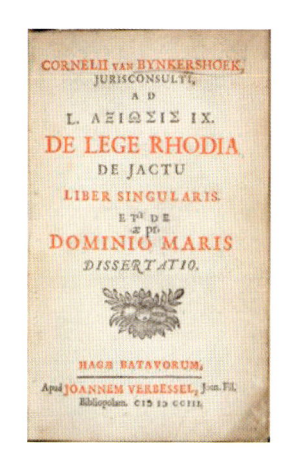

During the 1930 *Hague Codification Conference*, under the auspices of the League of Nations, efforts were made to reach agreement on the width of the territorial sea. A majority supported a three-mile territorial sea, but no general agreement could be reached. Between 1930 and 1958, the year in which the first UN Conference on the Law of the Sea took place, strong pressure emerged in favour of a wider area of coastal State jurisdiction. Emphasis shifted from the sea as an avenue of transportation and communication to the sea as an important zone for the exploitation of natural resources. Consequently, the law of the sea's evolution shifted in the 20th century from a law of international transportation to a law of appropriation by States. The law of the sea was finally codified in four conventions signed in Geneva in 1958:
- Convention on the Territorial Sea and Contiguous Zone;
- Convention on the High Seas;

p. 70

- Convention on Fishing and Conservation of Living Resources of the High Seas;
- Convention on the Continental Shelf.

However, the ink on these conventions had scarcely dried before significant changes became apparent in the centuries-old law of the sea as codified in 1958. For example, most developing countries had obviously not participated in formulating the law of the sea. Furthermore, great technological advances now allowed not only exploitation of the continental shelf at greater depths (namely for oil and gas) but also of the deep seabed in mining operations. Moreover, overfishing and exhaustion of fish stocks became a real threat despite the *Fishing Convention* of 1958 calling for 'optimum sustainable yield'. These developments caused a number of coastal states (in particular Iceland and Latin American countries) in the 1960s to claim not only a broader territorial sea but also increasingly greater areas of the open sea as their own fishing zone. The trend towards declaring ever wider territorial seas culminated in the 200 mile-territorial sea first claimed by Chile, El Salvador and Panama. It was clear that the entire law of the sea needed to be revised. For this purpose, a third *Law of the Sea Conference* was convened by the United Nations in 1973 (the first had been in 1958, the second in 1960) which ultimately resulted in a substantially new and comprehensive convention in 1982. This convention lays down rules for virtually all possible uses of the sea

Poster for the World Oceans Day 2010

(shipping, fishing, the laying of pipes and cables, overflight, scientific research of the sea, etc.) as well as delimiting the various maritime zones. Due to its comprehensive nature and the universal participation, this convention is also referred to as the '*World Constitution of the Oceans*'.

> **Important phases in the development of the law of the sea:**
>
> * Mare liberum of Hugo Grotius, 1609
> * Customary international law
> * Four conventions of 1958
> * United Nations Convention on the Law of the Sea, 1982
> * Agreement relating to the implementation of Part XI of the United Nations Convention, 1994
> * Convention relating to the conservation and management of migratory fish stocks, 1995

3. World Constitution for the Seas and Oceans

Under the UN Convention on the Law of the Sea (UNCLOS) of 1982, every coastal state has a territorial sea of a maximum of 12 nautical miles measured from the baselines which are usually the low water lines. A nautical mile is approximately 1.8 km. A state has the same authority on its territorial sea that it has on land, while, however, the right of innocent passage must be recognised.

Furthermore, the coastal state has several special rights in the area of sea that is connected to its territorial waters known as the contiguous zone (up to 24 nautical miles from the coast). These rights include issues related to customs, fiscal, sanitary and immigration laws. In addition, public international law recognises the exclusive rights of coastal states to the continental shelf (the seabed that extends beyond its territorial sea where mineral resources such as gas and oil can be exploited). The drilling platforms on the continental shelf also fall under the sovereignty of the coastal state. Claims to exclusive national economic jurisdiction were first made by the American president Truman in the so-called Truman Proclamation: "Having concern for the urgency of conserving and prudently using its natural resources", the President stated that:

> "…the United States regards the natural resources of the subsoil and sea-bed of the continental shelf beneath the high seas but contiguous to the coasts of the United States as appertaining to the United States, subject to its jurisdiction and control."

These rights are now laid down in UNCLOS 1982 that entered into force in 1994. There is also provision for an Exclusive Economic Zone of 200 nautical miles (350 km) from the coast in which the coastal state has exclusive rights to the exploitation of the living (fish) and non-living (oil and gas) natural resources. Many states have incorporated these provisions in their national legislation. With respect to proper management and optimal use of migratory fish stocks, a special supplementary fisheries convention has been concluded in 1995.

On the high seas no sovereign rights may be exercised. They have remained global seas. Every state, according to traditional public law, has the right to sail on, fish in, fly over and lay cables in these waters as well as to exercise other freedoms recognised in customary international law. However, in the exercise of these rights and freedoms, states must take the reasonable interests of others into consideration. In many cases specific arrangements exist, for example for fishing, overflight and environmental protection.

Maritime Zones

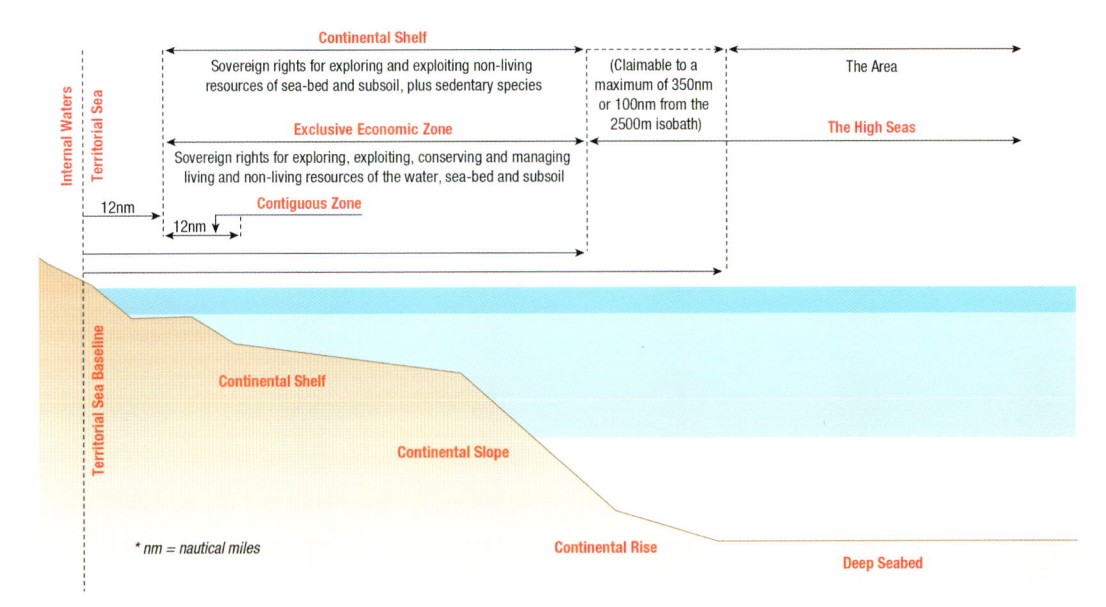

Continental Shelf
Sovereign rights for exploring and exploiting non-living resources of sea-bed and subsoil, plus sedentary species

(Claimable to a maximum of 350nm or 100nm from the 2500m isobath)

The Area

Exclusive Economic Zone
Sovereign rights for exploring, exploiting, conserving and managing living and non-living resources of the water, sea-bed and subsoil

The High Seas

Internal Waters
Territorial Sea
12nm

Contiguous Zone
12nm

Territorial Sea Baseline

Continental Shelf

Continental Slope

* nm = nautical miles

Continental Rise

Deep Seabed

Deep seabed exploitation or the testing or storage of nuclear weapons or other weapons of mass destruction do not belong to the recognised freedoms of the high seas. In the fundamental revision of the law of the sea, a new legal status for the deep seabed has been created based on the new principle of the 'common heritage of humankind'. The idea of freedom of exploitation of the deep seabed ('first come, first served'), is not consistent with the principles of international cooperation nor with taking into consideration the interests and needs of developing countries. Hence, developing countries urged the establishment of an international seabed authority which would govern exploitation. Part XI of the UNCLOS provides for a detailed international framework for deep sea mining. However, it is this part that has caused objections by a number of large, developed countries whereby the question arose as to whether this envisaged deep sea mining framework would ever be realised.

p. 21

After additional negotiations, an agreement on the implementation of Part XI of the Law of the Sea Convention was finally adopted on 28 July 1994. This agreement provides for an International Seabed Authority that manages the seabed on behalf of all humankind. The authority is an autonomous organization that oversees the activities of the parties to the Law of the Sea Convention which are related to the seabed in areas outside national jurisdictions. This includes the administration of natural resources and the issuing of permits for their exploitation. In recent years the question of who is liable for the environmental consequences which may result from deep seabed exploitation arose. The International Tribunal for the Law of the Sea (ITLOS) issued its first Advisory Opinion on this issue on 11 February 2011, at the request of the island state Nauru which considered to serve as a sponsoring state of the activities multinational mining companies. Meanwhile, there has been virtually no actual deep seabed exploitation due to the enormously high costs involved and the relatively low prices of minerals at the world market.

Dispute Concerning Delimitation of the Maritime Boundary between Ghana and Côte d'Ivoire in the Atlantic Ocean (Ghana/Côte d'Ivoire), ITLOS.

4. Settlement of international maritime disputes

In addition to issuing advisory opinions, the *International Tribunal for the Law of the Sea* (with its seat in Hamburg) is responsible for settling disputes between States on the interpretation and application of the international law of the sea. In the fifteen years of its existence, the tribunal has principally sat on cases concerning the seizure of ships which – whether or not they sailed under a foreign or cheap flag (so-called flag of convenience) – were suspected of, for example, illegal fishing activities. A remarkable, unique 'global competence' of the tribunal is that it can act as guardian of the general interest in the protection of the marine environment though this competence is limited as a state must first bring a case against another state before the tribunal. Of course, exceptions are its advisory opinions. In addition to the one on deep seabed mining mentioned above, ITLOS rendered on 2 April 2015 a second advisory opinion on IUU fishing, that is 'illegal, unreported and unregulated'. It did so upon request of the regional fisheries commission of seven West African States which were deeply concerned by such fishery activities by flags of convenience vessels in their EEZs.

Did you know that ...

At the International Tribunal for the Law of the Sea developing countries that are parties to a dispute before the tribunal may qualify for financial assistance to help them cover some of the costs caused by the case, made available by a voluntary trust fund established by the United Nations General Assembly?

Established:	1994 (entry into force of UNCLOS)
Mandate:	adjudicate disputes arising out of the interpretation and application of UNCLOS
Jurisdiction:	all disputes and all applications submitted to it in accordance with UNCLOS
First case:	M/V "SAIGA" Case (Saint Vincent and the Grenadines v. Guinea)
Number of cases:	25
Composition:	21 judges from different nationalities
State Parties:	166 plus the EU
Official Languages:	English and French
Website:	https://www.itlos.org/

The Arctic Sunrise in the Arctic Sea.

As regards disputes between states, on 22 November 2013 the ITLOS ordered temporary measures in a case between the Netherlands and Russia in relation to the ship Arctic Sunrise. In September 2013, the Russian coastguard boarded the Greenpeace ship, which sailed under the Dutch flag, and took it to the harbour of Murmansk. The Arctic Sunrise was in the Barents Sea to protest against the Russian oil platform Prirazlomnaya that was being used to drill for oil in the environmentally fragile Arctic area. This oil platform is situated in the exclusive economic zone in which Russia, as the relevant coastal state, has sovereign rights to the exploration and exploitation of any natural resources present. The Netherlands and Russia are both party to the UNCLOS. Upon ratification of the convention in 1996, the Netherlands chose the International Court of Justice as the body to settle any disputes while on the occasion of its ratification in 1997 Russia opted for an Annex VII Tribunal or an Annex VIII Tribunal (for cases of dispute over fishing, environmental pollution, sea research or shipping). In such a case of different choices of court, a special tribunal (the so-called Annex VII Tribunal) is the mandatory fallback procedure. The Netherlands applied to ITLOS for a sort of temporary ruling, in light of the urgency of the situation. As

Russia did not respond to the Netherlands request to submit the case to an arbitration procedure and in fact formally placed the ship under embargo and, moreover, held the crew prisoner, the Netherlands, after the prescribed waiting period of two weeks, requested that ITLOS issue temporary measures. These measures included the immediate release of the ship and allowing it to leave Russian territorial waters and resume the freedom afforded to shipping, the release of all crew members and that all judicial and administrative procedures against the ship and the crew be suspended pending the arbitration procedure. On 22 November 2013, ITLOS assented to virtually all of these demands. However, Russia continued to deny that the court had jurisdiction in the case. Not until just before Christmas 2013 did President Putin grant amnesty to the crew and the ship Arctic Sunrise was eventually released in June 2014. In view of Russia's non-acceptance of ITLOS or ICJ as the courts for dispute settlement in this case, the special tribunal was created to judge on the case. Once again Russia refused to appear and to participate. Notwithstanding this, the arbitral tribunal rendered on 14 August 2015 its final award which in essence confirms the earlier findings of ITLOS and found Russia to be acting in violation of UNCLOS and to be liable for the damage and suffering caused to the Arctic Sunrise and its crew.

Captain of the Arctic Sunrise, Peter Wilcox, taken into custody by the Russian border guards

These maps from the 1969 ICJ judgment in the case on the North Sea Continental Shelf (Federal Republic of Germany/Netherlands) show clearly the maritime delimitation on the North Sea.

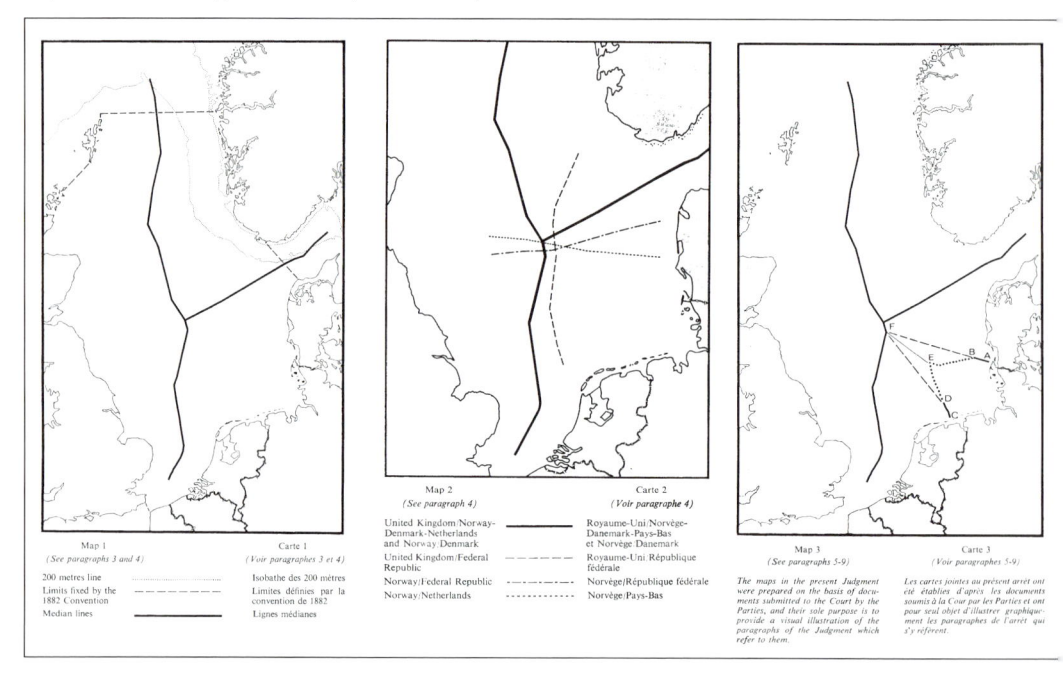

The *International Court of Justice* (ICJ) has also been actively engaged in the settlement of various maritime disputes. These relate, first of all, to questions of delimitation, such as boundary disputes over land, islands and rocks and their adjacent marine areas over which two or more States claim sovereignty or sovereign rights. A landmark case in this category is the *North Sea Continental Shelf Case* (1969), in which the ICJ underscored the firm status of coastal States' rights with respect to the continental shelf and delimited the North Sea continental shelf among the Netherlands, Germany and Denmark.

A second category relates to the various rights and obligations arising from the law of the sea. For example, the ICJ hears disputes relating to the use of the seas and oceans, especially interference with certain freedoms and rights such as (traditional) fishing rights or rights of 'innocent passage' and manoeuvring by naval vessels. Here reference can be made to the first case of the ICJ, the Corfu Channel case (*Great Britain v. Albania*) in which the Court held Albania responsible for not warning the British navy of the existence of mines in the Corfu Channel with the explosion of mines in Albanian waters causing loss of human life and damage to British naval vessels. The *Anglo-Norwegian Fisheries Case* (1951) and the Fisheries Jurisdiction Cases (*UK v. Iceland; FRG v. Iceland*, 1974) also fit into this category.

A third category concerns disputes on the use and management of shared resources, such as oil and gas fields or fish stocks which expand or migrate respectively over two EEZs or an EEZ and the high seas. The latter was an issue in the case of *Canada v. Spain* before the Court, which was finally settled out of court in view of the exclusive EU competency in the field of fisheries.

A fourth category is the conservation and preservation of the marine environment. This was one of the principal issues in the ICJ advisory opinion procedure on the *Legality of the Use or Threat of Nuclear Weapons* (1996).

A fifth and last category relates to the management of natural resources of the high seas and sea-bed. An example in this category is the Whaling in the Antarctic Case which Australia (supported by New Zealand) instituted at the ICJ against Japan, resulting in a Court order for Japan in 2014 to immediately halt its whaling activities in the Southern Pacific and Antarctic waters.

p. 62

Corrado Giaquinto, Allegory of Peace and Ju

Outlook

After writing this book and discussing it with a range of people (who are listed in the acknowledgements), we come in the end to what is overall an optimistic conclusion. This optimism is underscored when we look at developments through historical eyes, seeing "where we have come from." To take but two examples, the 1899 Hague Peace Conference made it clear that states should resolve their conflicts not by fighting but through arbitration; and before the 1970s almost no one thought in terms of international agreements on environmental issues. We, the authors of the present book, do agree that sometimes an optimistic outlook is needed to see such progress and not to take easy refuge in the negative hypes of the moment. As to the UN, international organization *par excellence* for the development and enforcement of international law, we should also not overlook that it is often asked to take action in difficult situations where governments are no longer able to find solutions. In that regard, it is also important in our view to not mix global legal cooperation, as practiced in the UN, with the (partly) supranational powers of an organization like the European Union. During the finalization of this book the new UN Secretary-General, António Guterres of Portugal, was appointed. The UN, starting in 1945 with fifty-one member states and expanding to 193 today, is an intergovernmental organization with a huge variety among its member countries in terms of political systems, from democratic to authoritarian, and with endless views on numerous topics. This is the reality we need to bear in mind as we talk about further developing international law and the role the UN should and can play in enforcing it. It also is our strong belief that one has to avoid the temptation and risk of considering some UN member states and some views *a priori* as good or bad. Here again, it makes sense to look through historical eyes. Consider for instance the position in the international arena of states such as Iran or Myanmar, moving from outsiders targeted by sanctions to trading partners. On a more abstract level, it can fairly be argued that without the UN and its many efforts to resolve problems by nonmilitary, law-driven, and law-inspired approaches, we would be back in the Middle Ages, with states conducting numerous wars, fighting for bigger territories and the like. In the end, we are optimistic about the role of international law, private and public, in addressing issues that at first sight might seem to be beyond human control. The UN as an organization and international law as a domain can no doubt be seen as part of the civilization of relations between states. However, we need to be careful to not overestimate the power of law. Rude power politics will remain, most likely forever. In addition, what seems to be safe today might not be safe anymore tomorrow.

As far as the role of international law is concerned in tackling major challenges, be it on the national or the international level, it is essential to not speak of international law as an indivisible whole, but to have a careful look at each of the subfields of international law. The enforcement mechanisms and possibilities as well as the enforcement itself vary from domain to domain, be it peace and security, trade, human rights, or any other field. What is needed is an understanding of the state of the art and the trends in international law, per domain as well as to international law 'at large', with an open mind as to historical developments and the geopolitical contexts in which progress must be realized.

Difficult discussions on issues such as the sovereignty of states are then inevitable and unavoidable. Although the concept is still key for the international community of states, and rightly so to our mind, it is also clear that the concept is challenged, either because "major problems have no passport" (Kofi Annan) – think of climate change – or because governments by and large do not take the interests of their populations as a starting point. This failure can be typified here as "sovereignty as responsibility" – internally between leadership and the population, externally in addressing major common problems. When it comes to common threats, states need to recognize, and are overall doing so more and more, that sovereignty can exist only through cooperation. The days of full and absolute sovereignty no longer exist, certainly not in light of the host of international law obligations that nowadays qualify state sovereignty. Nearly every chapter of this book provides examples.

Looking at international law in a reflective way, we basically see three trends. The first relates to the ongoing humanization of the international legal order, human rights for all being *the* lodestar, aspects of that being further integrated step by step in other domains of international law and in international relations. In the end, this evolution is about "conquering terrain upon rude power politics," which is what law makes law. In adopting and enforcing legal obligations and through various nonjudicial efforts, the world is shifting its primary focus from state security to human security.

Second, we see a new social contract emerging among states, the civil society (NGOs, trade unions, churches), and companies, supported and critically followed by the scientific community. The emphasis of the social contract is these days less on 'natural law' as it was during the Enlightenment, but rather on compulsory standards of international law the world agrees on. Think again of genocide, crimes against humanity and war crimes, and, for instance, the right to food and clean drinking water. Large portions of such standards are already incorporated in existing international law, while at the same time documents that are not legally binding come to mind, such as the Sustainable Development Goals adopted by the UN in September 2015. They include amongst other things goal number 16 on "peace, justice and strong institutions." Adoption of the Goals acknowledges once more that states cannot accomplish everything on their own, and that they need to join their efforts tackling the major challenges of the present era.

Stating this, we want to underscore once more, thirdly, the many reasons to embrace global cultural and political diversity. This is in line with vested concepts in the domain of international law such as 'consent to be bound', 'complementarity', 'subsidiarity', 'margin of appreciation', and 'respect for local particularities', as discussed in this book as well, while, however, not overlooking the also existing compulsory parts of international law. In other words: Understanding and taking diversity as a starting point and seeing the development of international law as an ongoing process with specific characteristics within each and every legal sub-domain, does not mean closing our eyes to violations of international law that need to be tackled in the immediate interests of affected populations. Doing that would be a sign of cultural relativism or even cynicism we would not accept.

In conclusion, we believe that one should always try to resolve the issues presented in this book by using legal means and methods, as well as any nonviolent approaches that might be available and effective. Think of roundtables, negotiations, mediation, involvement of special UN envoys, and basically anything that might help prevent conflicts and problems from becoming breaking news.

About the Authors

Prof. Dr. Willem van Genugten

Until recently, Willem van Genugten has been a full professor of International Law at Tilburg University, The Netherlands. As of now, he still holds a small chair in International Law at the North-West University, South Africa. Further to that he is, amongst other things, one of the Editors-in-Chief of the Netherlands Yearbook of International Law, chair of the Royal Netherlands Society of International law, chair of the Knowledge Platform Security and the Rule of Law of the Dutch government and chair of the Committee on the Implementation of the Rights of Indigenous Peoples of the International Law Association. He is the author of a long list of academic as well as popularizing publications in the field of international law. In 2012, he received a doctorate *honoris causa* from the North-West University in South Africa.

Daniela Heerdt, PhD candidate

In 2014 Daniela Heerdt graduated cum laude from her LL.M. in International and European Public Law at Tilburg University, with a specialization in international law and human rights. From February 2014 to December 2015 she has been working at Tilburg Law School to co-author this book. In February 2016, she took a teaching position for public international and European law at Utrecht University. From September 2016 onwards she is a PhD candidate at Tilburg Law School and conducts research in the field of business and human rights.

Prof. Dr. Nico Schrijver

Nico Schrijver is Professor of Public International Law and Academic Director of the Grotius Centre for International Legal Studies, Leiden University and a Senator in the

Dutch house of parliament where he chairs the Standing Committee on Foreign Affairs, Defence and Development Co-operation. Furthermore, he serves as independent expert member on the UN Committee on Economic, Social and Cultural Rights and is member of the Royal Netherlands Academy of Arts and Sciences, the Permanent Court of Arbitration and the Institut de droit international. From 2010-2012 he was the President of the International Law Association and from 2003-2011 the chair of the Royal Netherlands Society of International Law. Nico Schrijver is the author of Sovereignty over Natural Resources. Balancing rights and duties (Cambridge: CUP, 1997), The Evolution of Sustainable Development in International Law (Leiden: Brill, 2008) and Development without Destruction. The UN and Global Resource Management (Bloomington: IUP, 2010).

Index

A

Aboriginals	186
acta jure gestionis	68
ad hoc consent	57
Ad Hoc criminal tribunals	140
adaptation	161
advisory opinion	59
advisory opinion ICJ Kosovo	188
African Union (AU)	149
Agreement on Trade Related Aspects of Intellectual Property Rights (TRIPS)	129
Agreement relating to the implementation of Part XI of the United Nations Convention	201
Al-Bashir	150
American Convention on Human Rights	85
Anglo-Norwegian Fisheries Case	209
annulment of a contract	76
anticipatory self-defense	34
apostille	71
Aquinas, Thomas	25
Arab Charter on Human Rights	85
Arab Spring	22
arbitration	48
advantage of-	48
critique on-	53
legally binding	48
Arctic Sunrise	206
Argentina	62
armed conflict	45
Article 2 Charter of the United Nations	31, 45
Article 33 Charter of the United Nations	46
Asser, Tobias	26, 29, 70
Asser Institute, T.M.C.	29
Association of Southeast Asian Nations (ASEAN)	126
Australia v. Japan case	62
authorization of the use of force	32

B

Baby Gammy	90
Bern Convention for the Protection of Literary and Artistic Works	129
Bijnkershoeck, Cornelis van	198
biological weapons	21
Blackwater	190
bogus marriage	92
border-crossing terrorism	19
Boutros-Ghali, Boutros	10
breach of contract	75
Bretton Woods	107, 115
BRICS countries	108, 162
Brundtland report	166
Brussels I Regulations	72
Brussels I-bis Regulations	72, 74
Brussels II-bis Regulations	72, 74, 83
Budapest Convention on Cybercrime	122

C

Canada v. Spain case	209
Cancun Conference of the Parties	162
cannon shot rule	198
Carnegie, Andrew	51
Carnegie Foundation	51
Caroline doctrine	34
Cassin, René	179
certified emission reduction credits (CER)	164
Charter of Economic Rights and Duties	114
Charter of the United Nations	31
Article 2	31
Article 33	46
obligations	31
principles	31
chemical weapons	21, 39
child abduction	71, 85
child pornography	38
child protection	71
child sexual exploitation	123
child's best interest principle	85
Choice of Court Convention	73, 78
choice of law	75
in international contracts	112
principle	132
CIMIC Center of Excellence	35
civil partnership	94
civil war	19

Clean Development Mechanism (CDM)	164
Climate Change Liability	170
Climate Law	157
Code of EU Online Rights	133
Codification Conference	70
collective security	35
combatants	138
common but differentiated responsibility (CBDR)	166
common heritage of humankind	203
companies and human rights	190
compliance	37, 63
comprehensive sanctions	33
compromis	57
compulsory jurisdiction	57
compulsory licensing	105
conciliation	47
conflict	45
conflict prevention	37
conservation and preservation of the marine environment	209
contiguous zone	201
continental shelf	201
Convention for the Pacific Settlement of International Disputes	49
Convention on Choice of Court Agreements	73
Convention on Fishing and Conservation of Living Resources of the High Seas	200
Convention on Genocide	180
Convention on Jurisdiction, Applicable Law, Recognition, Enforcement and Co-operation in respect of Parental Responsibility and Measures for the Protection of Children	87
Convention on Parental Responsibility and Protection of Children	87
Convention on the Continental Shelf	200
Convention on the Elimination of All Forms of Discrimination against Women	84
Convention on the High Seas	199
Convention on the Law Applicable to Matrimonial Property Regimes	77
Convention on the Prohibition of Development, Production, Stockpiling, and Use of Chemical Weapons and Their Destruction	39
Convention on the Recognition of Registered Partnerships	95
Convention on the Rights of the Child	84
Convention on the Territorial Sea and Contiguous Zone	199
Convention against Torture	180
Convention relating to the Conservation and Management of Migratory Fish Stocks	201
Copyright Treaty	129
copyrights	129
Cordonnier, Louis	51
Corfu Channel case	208
Council of Europe	182
Covenant on the League of Nations	178
Creative Commons (CC)	130
crime of aggression	147
crime of sexual violence	151
crime of terrorism	144
crimes against humanity	138, 147, 150
cross-border crime	20
customary international law	61
Cybercrime	38, 120
Cybercrime	
Europol	121
fight against-	122
Interpol	123
investigation	121
jurisdiction	120
Cybercrime@Octopus	122

D

Darfur	150
Darknet	121
Data Protection Directive	126
De dominio maris dissertatio	198
De Jure Belli Ac Pacis	101
De Jure Praedae Commentarius	101
Declaration on Fundamental Principles and Rights at Work	192

Declaration on the Permanent Sovereignty over Natural Resources	113
Declaration on the Rights of Indigenous Peoples	187
Decolonization Declaration	188
Deep seabed exploitation	203
deep seabed mining	205
Deep Web	121
diplomacy	37
diplomatic methods of dispute settlement	46
diplomatic relations	55
diplomatic sanctions	33
Directive on Enforcement of Intellectual Property Rights	129
Directive on Copyright in the Information Society	129
dissenting opinion	59
divorce and legal separation	83
domestic violence	82
drones	21
drug trafficking	38

E

East-Timor	144
eBay	133
ebola	23
e-commerce	132
economic sanctions	33
emission of greenhouse gases	159
emission trading system	164
enforcement of international law	31
Enlightenment	177
enquiry	47
equal treatment of women	92
European Convention on Human Rights	85, 126
European Court of Human Rights	63, 126, 182
European Court of Justice	33, 131
European Cybercrime Centre (EC3)	123
European Organized Crime Threat Assessment	38
European Patent Office	106
European Union	72
family law	83
Europol	38
Europol Convention	38

Exclusive Economic Zone	202
external self-determination	187

F

family life	82, 84
Federal Bureau of Investigation (FBI)	121
female genital mutilation	183
financial crime	38
Fishing Convention	200
flag of convenience	205
food security	159
forced pregnancy	152
forum non conveniens doctrine	74
forum prorogatum	57
Four Freedoms	31
speech	178
fraud marriage	92
freedom of expression	128
freedom of the high seas	198
French Declaration of the Rights of Man and of the Citizen	177
FRG v. Iceland case	209

G

G20	108
gender based persecution	152
General Agreement on Tariffs and Trade	102
General Assembly	60
General Comments	181
General Data Protection Regulation	126
General Treaty for the Renunciation of War	28
Geneva Conventions	139
genocide	138, 147, 150
Global Conference on Cyberspace	122
global economic law	102
global warming	158
Google Spain's liability	132
Grotius, Hugo	25, 101, 102, 198
Group of Seven (G7)	108
Guidelines for Multinational Enterprises	192
Guiding Principles on Business and Human Rights	192

H

habitual residence	68
Hague Adoption Convention	88, 92
Hague Codification Conference	199
Hague Conference on Private International Law	69, 70
Hague Conference on Private International Law	82
Hague Convention on Celebration and Recognition of the Validity or Marriages	95
Hague Convention on Civil Procedure	69
Hague Convention on Protection of Children and Co-operation in Respect of Intercountry Adoption	88
Hague Convention on the Civil Aspects of International Child Abduction	85
Hague Convention on the Laws of War and War Crimes	27
Hague Peace Conferences	178
Hague Principles on Choice of Law in International Commercial Contracts	76
Hague Protocol on Law Applicable to Maintenance Obligations	77
Hague Regulations	139
Helsinki Principles	37
High Commissioner on National Minorities	37, 188, 189
Hippo, Augustine of	25
human dignity	175
human rights law	175
climate change and-	169
Human Rights Council	47
human security	42
human trafficking	38
humanitarian intervention	41

I

ICC Review Conference	147
illegal drug trade	20
illegal immigration networks	38
ILO	192
inquiry	47
Inspection Panel	116
intellectual property	129
Inter-American Commission on Human Rights	169
intercountry adoption	71, 82, 88
Intergovernmental Panel on Climate Change (IPCC)	158
intermediaries	131
international dispute settlement	45
international family law	81
treaties	84
international economic law	99
International Adult Protection	92
international arbitration	48
International Bank for Reconstruction and Development (IBRD)	115
International Centre for the Settlement of Investment Disputes (ICSID)	109
international child protection challenges in-	85
international child relocation and placement	82
international commercial arbitration	48
international commercial law	111
International Commission on Civil Status	95
International Convention on the Elimination of All Forms of Racial Discrimination	58
International Convention on the Protection of the Rights of All Migrant Workers and Members of Their Families	84
International Court of Justice	55, 56
admissibility	58
interim or provisional measures	58
jurisdiction	57
law-making role	60
maritime cases	208
Nicaragua case	34
organization	59
proceedings	58
rulings	61
separate or dissenting opinion	59
Statute	55
International Covenant on Civil and Political Rights	84, 126

International Covenant on
  Economic, Social, and
  Cultural Rights   84
international crimes   138
International Criminal
  Court   63, 147, 148, 181
international criminal law   137
      achievements and
      challenges of-   151
International Criminal Tribunal
  for Rwanda (ICTR)   142
International Criminal Tribunal
  for the former
  Yugoslavia   140, 141, 181
International Development
  Association (IDA)   115
international divorce   92
international economic order   114
international enforcement of child
  support   82
international environmental law   157
international finance and
  investment law   107
International Finance
  Corporation   115
International Forum on
  Intercountry Adoption and
  Global Surrogacy   89
international humanitarian law   138
International Institute for the
  Unification of Private Law
  (UNIDROIT)   113
International Institute of
  Social Studies   89
international investment law   109
International Labour
  Organization   178
international law
      definition   7
      enforcement   31
      obligations   31
International Law of Sales and
  Contracts   111
international marriage   92
International Monetary Fund   107
International Organization for
  Migration (IOM)   186
international peace and security   19
International Society of Family Law   82
International Tribunal for the Law
  of the Sea (ITLOS)   204, 205

International Women's Movement   27
Interpol   137
Inuit   169, 186
investment treaties   109
Iran-US Claims Tribunal   52, 53
Islamic Legal Perspectives on
  Cross-Border Family Disputes
  Involving Children   87
Israeli Wall   60

J

Judgments Project   78
judicial review   57
just war concept   25

K

Kadi cases   33
Kant, Immanuel   177
Kellogg-Briand-Pact   28
Kenyatta, Uhuru Muigai   149
kin state   188
Kony, Joseph   153
Kosovo   188
Kyoto Protocol   162, 168

L

lack of uniformity   133
Law of the Sea   197
Law of the Sea Conference   200
Law of the Sea Convention   204
League of Nations   28, 55
      covenant   28
      codification conference   70
Lebanon   144
legal dispute
      definition   45
Legality of the Use or Threat
  of Nuclear Weapons   209
lex mercatoria   111
Libya   42
Locke, John   177
Lord's Resistance Army (LRA)   153
Lubanga Dyilo, Thomas   151
Lugano Convention   78

M

Magna Carta	177
Malta-Process	87
Mare liberum	198
margin of appreciation	183
maritime boundaries	55
maritime disputes	205
maritime zones	203
Marrakesh Accords	165
Martens Clause	25
Martens, Fyodor	25, 26
Masaai	186
mass surveillance	125
matrimonial property law	83
Measures Prohibiting the Importation and Marketing of Seal Products	104
mediation	47
merchant law	111
military intervention	33
Millennium Development Goals	114
Minsk II-peace agreement	22
mitigation	161
mixed tribunals	144
most favored nation	103
Multilateral Investment Guarantee Agency	115
multilateral trade negotiations	102

N

National Action Plans	193
National Security Agency (NSA)	124
national tort law	193
nautical mile	201
NCI Agency	35, 36
negotiation	46
New International Economic Order (NIEO)	113
Nicaragua case	34
Nigerian oil spill	193
non binding dispute settlement methods	46
non-combatants	138
nonproliferation	21
chemical weapons	39
Non-Proliferation Treaty	21
nonstate actors	
arbitration	48
North Atlantic Treaty Organization	35
North Sea Continental Shelf case	208
North-South debate	167
nullum crimen sine lege	138
Nuremberg Tribunal	139

O

obligations in international law	31
open source movement	130
opinio juris	61
Organisation for Economic Co-operation and Development (OECD)	133, 192
Organisation for Security and Co-operation in Europe (OSCE)	21, 37, 188
Organisation for the Harmonization of Business Law in Africa	73
Organisation for the Prohibition of Chemical Weapons	39
Organization of American States	73, 78
organized crime	20
Our Children's Trust	170

P

parallel litigation	74
Paris meeting on climate change	160
Paris Peace Conference	55
party autonomy	76
patents	105
Peace Palace	49, 51
peace through law movement	49
peaceful dispute settlement	45
peacekeeping	40
Permanent Court of Arbitration	48, 49, 109
Foundation	26
Permanent Court of International Justice	49, 55
polluter pays principle	167
post conflict peacebuilding	40
precautionary principle	166
preventive self-defence	34
principle	
comity	77
complementarity	147
free trade	104

intergenerational equity	170
nondiscrimination	103
principles	27
fair competition	103
permanent peace	27
reciprocity	103
transparency	103
prisoners of war	138
private international law	67
connecting factors	68
function of-	68
goal of-	68
jurisdiction	67, 73, 82
Recognition and Enforcement of Judgments	77
private military and security companies (PMSCs)	190
proportionality	138
prostitution	151
protecting innocent civilians under international law	41
protection of data	124
protection of privacy	124
protection of private life	127

R

R2P	42
Rana Plaza building	191
rape	151
refugees	185
registered partnership	83
Resolution 1973	42
Responsibility to Protect	42
right to development	167
right to freedom of speech	131
right to self-determination	60
Rio Declaration on Environment and Development	168
Rome Regulations	72, 77, 83
Roosevelt, Eleanor	179
Roosevelt, Franklin	31, 178
Rousseau, Jean-Jacques	177

S

same-sex	
couple	95
partnership	94

sanctions	
comprehensive	33
smart	33
targeted	33
Secretary-Generals of the United Nations	12
Security Council	32
members	32
resolution	33
Responsibility to Protect	42
self-defence	
preventive and anticipatory	34
self-determination	187
separate opinion	59
sexual slavery	151
sexual violence	152
Silk Road	121
smart sanctions	33
Snowden, Edward	125
social media	
role in conflicts	23
soft law instruments	76, 108
Special Court for Sierra Leone	143
Special Tribunal for Lebanon (STL)	144, 145
spill-over effects	23
state practice	61
state sovereignty	41
limits	183
stateless people	185
sterilization	152
subsidiarity principle	89
surrogacy	89
illegal-	91
surrogacy arrangements	88
sustainable development	166
Sustainable Development Goals	114
Syria	37
chemical weapons	40

T

targeted sanctions	33
Taylor, Charles	143
technology, international law and	119
territorial sovereignty	198
terrorism	20
definition	20
testamentary dispositions	71
The Agreement on Trade-Related Aspects of Intellectual Property Rights	105

The Hague
    Legal Capital   10
The Hague Academy of
    International Law   51
The Hague Climate Conference   163
The Hague Conference on Private
    International Law (HCCH)   111
        founding   29
The Hague Peace Conferences   25, 26
        First Conference   26
        Second Conference   27
        Third Conference   27
the right to be forgotten   131
threat of force   31
Tokyo Military Tribunal   139
torts   74, 75
trade in children   92
trade law   102
trafficking   152
Transatlantic Trade and Investment
    Partnership (TTIP)   110
Treaty of Berlin   178
Truman Proclamation   202
Tsar Nicholas II   26

U

UK v. Iceland case   209
Ukraine crisis   22, 37
        ICC and-   148
UN Commission on Human
    Rights   179
UN Commission on International
    Trade Law (UNCITRAL)   53, 111
UN Convention on the Law of
    the Sea (UNCLOS)   199, 201
UN Conference on Trade and
    Development (UNCTAD)   114
UN Convention on Contracts for
    the International Sale of Goods 111
UN Human Rights Council   179
UN human rights supervisory
    bodies   180
UN Mechanism for International
    Criminal Tribunals (MICT)   142
UNESCO   60
unilateral declaration   57
Union of Utrecht   177
United Kingdom's Government
    Communications Head Quarters
    (GCHQ)   125

United Nations
    founding   55
United Nations Framework
    Convention on Climate Change
    (UNFCCC)   161
United Nations Millennium
    Declaration   114
United Nations Refugee Agency
    UNHCR   186
United Nations security system   31
Universal Declaration of
    Human Rights   84, 126, 179
Universal Periodic Review (UPR) 183
universalization of human rights   184
Urgenda   171
Uruguay-Argentina case   62
Uruguay Round   102
US Bill of Rights   177
use of force   25, 31
        authorization   32
        ICJ   55
        self-defense   34

V

Vattenfall v. Germany   109
victims   152
Vienna World Conference on
    Human Rights   184

W

war crimes   138, 147, 150
weapons of mass destruction   21, 203
Whaling case   62, 209
WikiLeaks   130
Wikipedia   133
Windstream Energy LLC case   48
witness protection   152
World Bank
        Development and-   115
World Bank Group   115
World Congress on Family Law
    and Children's Rights   82, 84
World Constitution of the Oceans 201
World Health Organization   60
World Trade Organization   102, 105
        development and-   115

dispute settlement
   mechanism   63, 104
wrongful act of state   171
wrongful acts   63